JOURNEY TO FASHION DESIGN

College Admissions & Profiles

Rachel A. Winston, Ph.D.

ISBN 978-1946432551 (hardback); 978-1946432544 (paperback); 978-1946432568 (e-book)

LCCN: 2022903561

Lizard Publishing® 7700 Irvine Center Drive, Suite 800 Irvine, CA 92618 *www.lizard-publishing.com*

Lizard Publishing creates, designs, produces, and distributes books and resources to provide academic, admissions, and career information. Our mental process is fueled by three tenets:

- Ignite the hunger to learn and the passion to make a difference
- Illuminate the expanse of knowledge by sharing cutting edge thinking
- Innovate to create a world that makes the transition from dreams to reality

We work with academic leaders who transform the educational landscape to publish relevant content and advise students of their educational and professional options, with the aim of developing 21st-century learners and leaders. We also work with students to publish their books and present widely diverse ideas to the college/graduate school-bound community. With headquarters in Irvine, California, Lizard Publishing works virtually with authors to edit, publish, and distribute both hard copy and paperback books.

This book was published in the U.S.A. Lizard Publishing is a premium quality provider of educational reference, career guidance, and motivational publications/merchandise for global learners, educators, and stakeholders in education.

Book design by Michelle Tahan *www.michelletahan.com*

Book formatting by Obinna Chinemerem Ozuo

Book website: *www.collegefashionprograms.com*

LIZARD PUBLISHING

This book is dedicated to the talented and committed members of IECA with whom I have had the pleasure of working as a professional member for more than twenty-five years.

ACKNOWLEDGMENTS

There is never enough room to acknowledge every person. Numerous people contributed to my perspective about fashion design. Students, faculty, counselors, and researchers assisted in enhancing my knowledge base or taught me indelible lessons. Over a lifetime of experiences working with students, I am wiser and more worldly.

I gratefully acknowledge Michelle Tahan, Jasmine Jhunjhnuwala, E. Liz Kim, and Jacqueline Xu, as well as my family, friends, colleagues, and professors. It is with profound gratitude that I acknowledge those I have known in the fashion world.

As a faculty member in the UCLA College Counseling Certificate Program, I met many dedicated counselors who spend their life serving and supporting students. Meaningful contributions to the book have been made indirectly by admissions representatives, college counselors, faculty members who took a special interest in this book's success.

I would also like to thank the thousands of students I have taught, counseled, or supported in my nearly four decades of service.

Isaac Newton once said, "If I see so far, it is because I stand on the shoulders of giants."

"If I see so far, it is because I stand on the shoulders of giants."
– Isaac Newton

A few of those giants whose broad shoulders lifted me higher and helped teach invaluable lessons include: David Waugh, Roberta Mirvis, Sandy Greenspun, Harrison Woodruff, Taylor Devlin, Keyon Sabahi, Rodney Moradi, Ryan La, Sam Thompson, Sarah Huang, Kim Kelly, Colleen Ficco, Milton Daley, Emma Farkas, Austin Ferrero, Katie Foose, Nadia Kuba, and Paige Lundeen.

Finally, there would be no book on fashion design schools and no career college admissions counseling, without the support of Robert Helmer whose tireless efforts support me every single day.

ABOUT THE AUTHOR

Dr. Rachel A. Winston is a tireless student advocate. She has served the educational community as a university professor, college advisor, statistician, researcher, author, cryptanalyst, motivational speaker, publishing executive, and lifelong student. As one of the leading experts in college counseling and an award-winning faculty member, Dr. Winston has spent her lifetime learning, teaching, mentoring, and coaching students. Her counseling practice centers around college admissions, college essays, portfolios, and intellectual conversations about life and career pursuits

She started college at thirteen and graduated from college programs in such widely ranging disciplines as chemistry, mathematics, computers, liberal arts, international relations, negotiation, conflict resolution, peacebuilding, business administration, higher education leadership, interpreting, college counseling, and publishing. Throughout her education, she attended and graduated from Harvard, University of Chicago, GWU, UCLA, Syracuse, CSUF, CSUDH, Pepperdine, Claremont Graduate University, and Gallaudet University.

Her position working in Washington, D.C. on Capitol Hill and with the White House in the 1980s took her to approximately a hundred universities training campaign managers at colleges from Colorado to California, thoroughly dotting the western states. Later, she led college tours with students and their families on road trips throughout the United States. She has taught or counseled thousands of students over her career and speaks at conferences and academic programs throughout the world.

As a professor and avid writer for numerous publications, she won the 2012 McFarland Literary Achievement Award, Bletchley Park Cryptanalyst Award, and numerous other awards, including Faculty Member of the Year, Leadership Tomorrow Leader of the Year, and college service and leadership awards. While studying Human Capital at Claremont Graduate University, she was a scholarship recipient at the Drucker School of Management. She was also elected to the statewide Board of Governors for the Faculty Association for California Community Colleges, where she served on their executive committee.

She served as a faculty member for the UCLA College Counselor Certificate Program, the Director of Mathematics at Brandman University, and Embry Riddle Aeronautical University, Chapman University, Cal State Fullerton, and a handful of California Community Colleges, including Cerro Coso College where she also served as the Academic Senate President and retired in 2016. Over her career, she taught mathematics online, on television, live interactive satellite, telecourses, and in large and small lecture halls.

AUTHORS' NOTE

You are reading this book because you are considering admission to colleges where you open the doors to the world of fashion design. Whatever route you took to get to this point, you are in the right place. Right now, you need to gather information to make informed decisions.

While many people offer advice, suggestions differ. Friends will tell you the 'right' way or the way their neighbor was accepted. Graciously accept this anecdotal information while you commit to learning more. This opportunity to pursue fashion design is available so you can pursue your future.

Dig deeper to consider both expert and current information from counselors who have worked with hundreds of students. Changes in programs, curricula, requirements, and links happen each year.

Doublecheck each program's specifics yourself. This guide is current as of February 2022, with each school's profile information. However, since researching this book, changes may have taken place.

"We are what we think. All that we are arises with our thoughts. With our thoughts, we make the world."
— Buddha

There are other books about fashion design programs written by talented and experienced counselors. We admire and cheer on their efforts.

This information about colleges, admissions, profiles, and lists is different in that it also provides unique tidbits. We hope you find this information valuable. Your job is to begin early by assembling information for the schools you are considering. Create a road map and set yourself on a clear path.

If you see an error in this book or even a suggestion for a future edition, please write to Dr. Rachel A. Winston at collegeguide@yahoo.com. We will fix the entry with the next printed version. All of that said, this book was written for you in mind.

There is a wealth of information on the Internet with free downloads, FAQs, testimonials, and offers to help you with your applications. Some of these advisors are knowledgeable and can help you. Students and parents hunt around the web, searching for a tremendous number of hours to seek the information they need. We aim to resolve this problem.

This book with college admissions data and profiles was designed to make your search easier. For now, though, we will assume you want to attend school for fashion design and are exploring this avenue as a possible way to take advantage of a program to get you on your way toward your goal.

We assume that you are a talented candidate who is willing to work very hard. You may be fascinated with fashion, branding, advertising, e-commerce, or retail. Serving others selflessly is virtually a prerequisite for fashion design programs.

As you investigate colleges, you might find that some programs are listed in different college departments; either way, this book will help you reach your goal. Applying to and writing essays for each application will require research to determine which is right for you.

While you might believe that fashion design programs are relatively similar, each program's nuances make them very different. These small differences may seem confusing. My goal with this book is to demystify the information and process.

CONTENTS

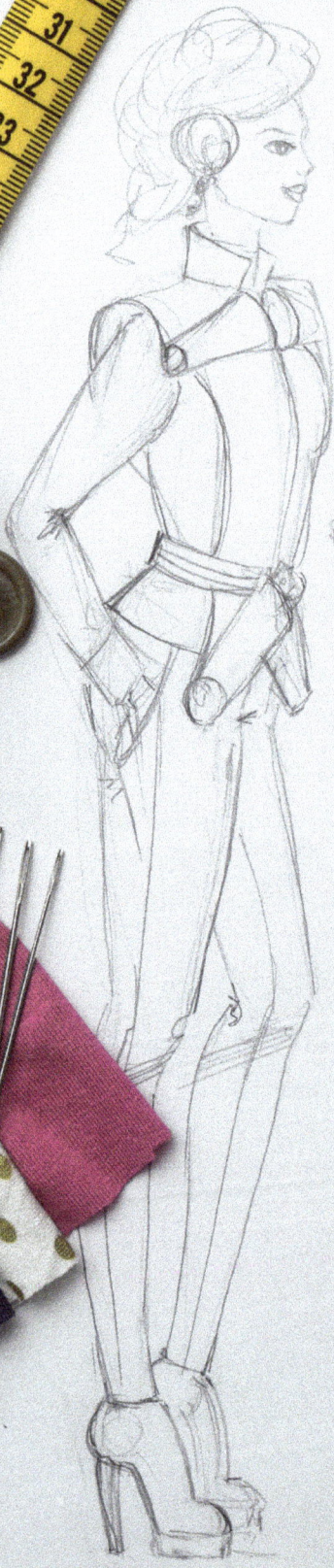

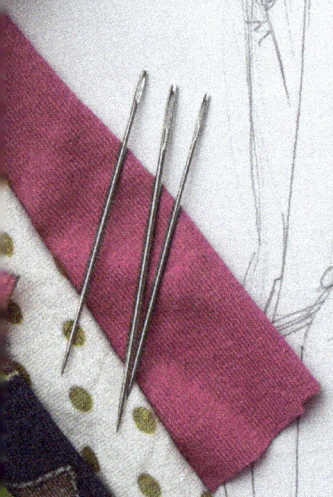

CHAPTER 1

FASHION SENSE: DESIGNING OUTFITS TO FIT INDIVIDUAL PERSONALITIES

"What I find most interesting in fashion is that it has to reflect our time. You have to witness your own moment."

– Nicolas Ghesquière

THE WORLD OF FASHION DESIGN

Enter a whole new world. Sometimes magical, sometimes mystical, sometimes mysterious, fashion design piques the interest of creatives who hunger to develop successful fashion brands, produce trendy clothing, envision costumes for theatre, work for a famous designer, or spare the environment of destructive, unsustainable fast fashion. College programs in fashion design combine the technology of sewing and patternmaking with the forward-thinking proficiencies in materiality, fashionomics, sustainability, techstyle, and societal impact. The world of fashion design awaits your entrance on the runway of fascination and excitement.

From imagination to drawings, students begin to envision a future in which they can influence, impress, and affect the future of apparel development, manufacturing, and distribution. Fashion is an art. Fresh, original ideas are always welcome. Furthermore, since everyone wears clothing, the demand is constant. For many people, individuality is important and style is everything.

From bathing suits and undergarments to haute couture and glamorous accessories, collections are produced for a targeted market space. Fashion designers must be able to communicate ideas, expressing them clearly in both visual and written text. For example, ready-to-wear designer and standard garments are suitable for large-scale manufacturing, though designer collections are higher in quality and thus have a different audience.

Artistic and creative, fashion design students span the spectrum of ideologies and perspectives. Expressiveness shines through sketches and tailoring. Knowing how to tailor, cut, drape, and sew are essential. Fashion design students must understand the basics of art, coloring, and design, while also knowing various fabrics, textile manufacturing, and quality fibers. Technology-driven students may be interested in the newly developed arena of techstyle, wearables, and digital clothing. Whether you are interested in textiles, design, knitting, embroidering, footwear, or accessories, there is a place for you.

Ultimately, whatever you design needs to be marketable. Ask questions. Who is your audience? What is their lifestyle? How do they interact in the social and professional arena? Thus, fashion design students must understand the economic, social, historical, political, and environmental landscape of people's consciousness. Read the news and watch trending demands. These images can conjure ideas that you can turn into your enduring fashion design.

PARADIGM SHIFTS

Paradigm shifts have rocked the fashion industry since the pandemic. From 2020 to 2022, the fashion industry was pummeled with changing interests, supply chain disruptions, and lack of demand. Social media changed the way people purchase items with the retail industry being the hardest hit. Consumers had new priorities. E-commerce boomed with buyers wanting touchless purchase options and social media marketers firing away posts at lightning speeds. Socially and environmentally conscious consumers took to the waves searching for sustainable wear and eco-friendly fashions.

Instagram, TikTok, YouTube, Twitter, Facebook, and Pinterest were some of the trending sites stimulating the interest in purchasers looking for their unique style. New fashion designers sprung up, watered by the pandemic's showers. As these seedlings grew, inconsistency emerged in quality, price, and deliverability.

In the digital-led world of fashion consumerism, fashion bloggers now play a key role in influencing purchases both on an objective quality level and a subjective, values-based level.

According to the McKinsey report, *State of Fashion 2022*, "The fashion industry posted a 20 percent decline in revenues in 2019-20" with obvious performance inequalities. "A record 69 percent of companies were value destroyers in 2020," compared to "28 percent in 2011. About 7 percent of companies left the market entirely, either due to financial distress or because they were bought by rivals."[1]

CELEBRITY FASHION BRANDS

Celebrities often turn their fashion sense into a brand. Headliners regularly promote jewelry, cosmetics, and clothing in the online and retail market space. Newcomers are welcomed too. In 2022, John Legend announced that he was joining with A-Frame Brands to create a skincare line for people of color. Beyonce ventured into the business space with her label Ivy Park; she now owns the company, running her own business. Khloé Kardashian took the fashion scene by storm. Her brand, Good American, offers curve-enhancing denim and activewear.

Some brands initially exploded, like Jessica Simpson, whose shoe line launched in 2006, making over $1 billion in revenue, far surpassing expectations. Reese Witherspoon's Draper James offers Southern-style, reaching a wide range of sizes and customers. In 2022, Fabletics, Kate Hudson's athleisure line, had 74 stores, 200 million VIP members, and $500 million in annual sales.

1   McKinsey & Company, "State of Fashion 2022: An Uneven Recovery and New Frontiers," *McKinsey & Company,* 2022, https://www.mckinsey.com/industries/retail/our-insights/state-of-fashion

The Row, a minimalist luxury brand, developed by the Olsen twins took off early. Teen superstars, Mary-Kate and Ashley created award-winning trendy garments worn by A-listers. Meanwhile, Victoria Beckham re-invigorated her transformational slim and sexy monochromatic clothing line, Victoria, Victoria Beckham. After the pandemic's tsunami, celebrity brands revived at global fashion bonanzas.

A-listers joined Paris Fashion Week 2022 with Charlotte Casiraghi riding down the catwalk on a horse during Chanel's exhibition. Celebrities included Naomi Campbell, Tyler, the Creator, Venus Williams, Kanye West, Julia Fox, Pharrell Williams, Victor Cruz, J. Balvin, Luka Sabat, Heron Preston, Evan Mock, Blake Cray, Noah Bech, Philippine Leroy-Beaulieu, Dave Chappelle, Cara Delevingne, Claire Foy, Rosamund Pike, and Camille Rowe, among many others.[2] The 2022 Milan Fashion Week runways were also abuzz in a sign that the fashion industry was on its way toward getting back to normal.

2022 TOP 30 FASHION BRANDS:[3]

1. Gucci - Italy
2. Dior - France
3. Nike - USA
4. Louis Vuitton - France
5. Prada - Italy
6. Balenciaga - Spain
7. Moncler - Italy
8. Bottega Veneta - Italy
9. Yves Saint Laurent - France
10. Versace - Italy
11. Fendi - Italy
12. Burberry – U.K.
13. Off-White - Italy
14. Alexander McQueen – U.K.
15. Valentino - Italy
16. Loewe - Spain
17. Givenchy - France
18. Balmain - France
19. Jacquemus - France
20. Rick Owens - USA
21. Stone Island - Italy
22. Dolce & Gabbana - Italy
23. Fear of God - USA
24. Raf Simons - Belgium
25. Vetements - Switzerland
26. Thom Browne – U.K.
27. Cartier - France
28. Rolex - Switzerland
29. Hermes - France
30. Armani – Italy

2   Tori Schneebaum, "All the celebrities at Paris Fashion Week 2022: Julia Fox, Kanye West, more," *Page Six*, January 25, 2022, https://pagesix.com/2022/01/25/all-the-celebrities-at-paris-fashion-week-2022/#25

3   Mandy Meyer, "Top Fashion Brands In The World In 2022 (30 Most Valuable & Popular)," *The Vou*, January 12, 2022, https://thevou.com/fashion/top-fashion-brands/

TOP FIVE COSMETIC/SKINCARE BRANDS FOR 2022[4]

Ranked by Money.co.uk

Cosmetics

1. Huda Beauty, 49.7 million Instagram followers, 29.8 million Instagram hashtags
2. Kylie Cosmetics, 25.4 million Instagram followers, 4.9 million Instagram hashtags
3. Fenty Beauty, 10.2 million Instagram followers, 5.2 million Instagram hashtags
4. Jeffree Star Cosmetics, 6.4 million Instagram followers, 3.3 million Instagram hashtags
5. Florence by Mills, 2.6 million Instagram followers, 989,000 Instagram hashtags

Skincare Brands

1. Kylie Skin, 5.5 million Instagram followers, 385,000 Instagram hashtags
2. Fenty Skin, 1 million Instagram followers, 116,000 Instagram hashtags
3. Supergoop!, 477,000 Instagram followers, 56,000 Instagram hashtags
4. Humanrace, 203,000 Instagram followers, 864,000 Instagram hashtags
5. Kora Organics, 436,000 Instagram followers, 42,000 Instagram hashtags

PANDEMIC EMERGENCE: NO MORE BOREDOM

During the quarantine and lingering pandemic, people became bored with their clothing. Seeking uniqueness and style, individuals hunted for multicolored flair, fringe, puffy clothes, jumpsuits, bell-bottoms, and cutout garments. The vibrancy of color surprised those who became used to neutral colors and pajama pants.

Fall 2021 began the new wave of tiny trendy fashion apparel. "Meet the micro-mini skirt, a holdover from the going-out styles of the early to mid-aughts, worn by all the biggest names of that era: Paris Hilton, Nicole Richie, Britney Spears, and Lindsay Lohan among them. The style re-emerged and began picking up steam on

---

4   James Manso, "2022's Hottest Celebrity Beauty Brands, Ranked," *WWD*, January 22, 2022, https://wwd.com/beauty-industry-news/beauty-features/2022s-hottest-celebrity-beauty-brands-ranked-1235038190/

the runways earlier this year, when Miu Miu and Saint Laurent showed teeny skirts in embellished jewels and tweeds for fall 2021."[5]

FASHION DESIGN FOR THE METAVERSE

The metaverse added a new dimension for the fashion designer. According to Forbes, in 2022, video game skins offer fashion designers a $40 billion per year market space.[6] Creativity and flair will allow image creators to wow. While the trifecta of demand, software, and hardware are converging in the 3D video space, the metaverse stands prepared to change the way we live and work.

According to Grayscale Investments, the world's largest crypto asset manager, "The market opportunity for bringing the Metaverse to life may be worth over $1 trillion in annual revenue and may compete with Web 2.0 companies worth ~$15 trillion in market value today."[7] While the metaverse may seem futuristic and sci-fi-like, billions of people are flocking to this new space. Meanwhile, video games and the Internet are likely to be transformed into this new 3D universe.

5   Kristen Bateman, "Why the Micro-Mini Skirt is 2022's Biggest Fashion Statement," *W Magazine*, October 22, 2021, https://www.wmagazine.com/fashion/micro-mini-skirt-y2k-fashion-mcbling-history

6   Joseph DeAcetis, "NFTs, Metaverse and GameFi Are Changing Up the Fashion Business in 2022," *Forbes*, December 22, 2021, https://www.forbes.com/sites/josephdeacetis/2021/12/22/nfts-metaverse-and-gamefi-are-changing-up-the-fashion-business-in-2022/.

7   Michael Cohen, "Grayscale Says Metaverse Tech Sector May Generate $1T Annual Revenue in the Future," *MSN, Microsoft News*, November 28, 2021, https://www.msn.com/en-us/money/news/grayscale-says-metaverse-tech-sector-may-generate-1t-annual-revenue-in-the-future/ar-AARe6nZ.

Numbers tell the story. Digital entertainment is a vast market with statistics that surpass prognosticators projections. According to *FinancesOnline*, "There were 2.69 billion video game players worldwide in 2020. The figure will rise to 3.07 billion in 2023 based on a 5.6% year-on-year growth forecast. The global games market had $159.3 billion in revenues for 2020, almost half of which came from the Asia Pacific market."[8]

To put this into perspective. One-third of the global population plays video games. While approximately two-thirds of residents in the United States play video games, this only comprises 15% of global gamers. What does this mean for digital creatives? If 85% of gamers live in other countries, geographical knowledge, cultural sensitivity, language acquisition will become increasingly valuable assets. There is a massive space for fashion designers with graphic design and advanced technology skills to jump on board. Furthermore, these numbers are destined to grow.

Generation Z and Millennials are investing in their education. Additionally, this group from 15 to 35 is expected to spend a trillion dollars on these technologies between 2022 and 2027. The once generic avatar skins and digital clothing styles are rapidly adapting to the new environment with styles that can quickly be updated from season to season. Creating personalized spaces, styles, and clothing, the metaverse's virtually enhanced physical and digital environment is set to provide social connections, amplifying the universe of the Internet. Video game and metaverse avatars will have personalized clothing without the need for manufacturing – a real game-changer, pardon the pun.

The environment is primed to attract customers to differentiated digital fashion brands. Big-name fashion brands like Dior, Gucci, Prada, Armani, and Miu Miu are some of the few companies with avatar branded garments. In addition, the video game, Fortnite, partnered with Balenciaga while Louis Vuitton partnered with League of Legends. Partnerships will increase as this avenue becomes more common. Popular virtual fashion specialists include XR Couture, The Fabricant, and DressX. Fashion brands are eager to attract young customers who will stay with them for life.

Marketing skills will become much more important to next-gen fashion designers as they target audiences to their business's core values. Consumer

---

8 "Number of Gamers Worldwide 2022/2023: Demographics, Statistics, and Predictions," *FinancesOnline*, accessed January 28, 2022, https://financesonline.com/number-of-gamers-worldwide/.

connectedness, social consciousness, and brand awareness will be even more important in these new digital environments. The creative and financial opportunities are virtually limitless. Fashion designers now have wide-ranging freedom to bring their fashions to life – literally. Along with a combination of cryptocurrencies and non-fungible tokens (NFTs), the purchasing power of Gen Zs and Millennials will drive the fashion train into the next station – the metaverse.

FASHION DESIGNERS WITH TECHNOLOGY SKILLS APPLY HERE

The fashion industry needs skilled workers. Technological skills continue to be in high demand. Companies search long and hard for applicants to fashion design jobs who also have digital marketing, cybersecurity, supply chain logistics, wearable technology, and STEM skills. To recover from the past few years of downturns, brands must upgrade and update their deliverables and enter the next frontier of digitization. Inflation and price increases will change industry dynamics. Competition for the best and brightest applicants with technology skills has never been greater.

"LIFE IS A JOURNEY, NOT A DESTINATION"

Ralph Waldo Emerson suggested that people avoid conformity, search for an inner conscience, and discover a sense of purpose along the way. Enjoy your journey.

CHAPTER 2

TECHNICAL SKILLS: PATTERN CONSTRUCTION, SEWING, AND GRAPHIC DESIGN

"I adore the challenge of creating truly modern clothes, where a woman's personality and sense of self are revealed. I want people to see the dress, but focus on the woman."

– Vera Wang

SEWING, FABRIC, AND PATTERN MAKING

While creative thinking is at the heart of fashion design, sewing is an essential skill. Not all designers know how to sew, but fashion designers must. Having these skills before entering college is incredibly valuable—almost a necessity. However, quick learners who put the time into becoming technically accurate and proficient at sewing will do fine provided all of their other design skills are solid.

In addition to using sewing machines and being comfortable with needle and thread stitching, fashion design students should be fluent in the various types of fabric. Naming fabric types and having a sense of types of threads and textiles is essential. Play with each type of fabric, test out stitching, flexibility, and durability. Some fabrics rip while others are so delicate that they run, pull, or cannot be easily used in garments. Try decorating elements - some work, some fall off.

Part of your college education will be devoted to practice, assessment, and experience. Read what other people have written about their experience with fabrics. Some work and some do not. Learn from others. Experience is a tough teacher, but one that is invaluable as you progress.

Pattern making is a key component, requiring arithmetic and geometry skills. Like experimenting with fabric, pick up a dozen patterns and attempt to make the items for yourself. Develop techniques to improve the pattern and the instructions. Instructions must be clear, so writing and accurate communication skills are a must.

SKETCHING AND GRAPHIC DESIGN

Sketching and graphic design are valuable skills for your long-term career pursuits. Draw out what you see in your mind. Take lessons to improve your drawing skills. Other people need to see what you envision.

Portfolios for fashion design admissions frequently require sketches, though not all fashion design schools require a portfolio. Sketching fashion design ideas allows others to visualize what you envision as your final outcome. Pattern making also requires drawing and graphic design skills.

You are likely to use digital design software during college like Adobe Creative Cloud (Photoshop, Illustrator, InDesign, Premiere Pro, Acrobat, etc.), AutoCAD, 3DS Max, Revit, or Sketchup. Others may be required at your school. Nevertheless, it is extremely helpful to have graphic design and digital software skills before entering college. Training before and during college is valuable in the long run, probably more so with technology integration into every aspect of our lives.

MAKEUP

While makeup design may not be taught in a college class, it is an indispensable component of a fashion photoshoot or a runway appearance. The technical details of makeup artistry are significantly more complicated than makeup you might purchase for every day wear.

First, the makeup applied to the face and body needs to last last through complex photo or video shoots that may require dancing or movement. Second, how makeup is applied and the designs created can be thoroughly artful. Third, applying makeup for photography or film requires different materials and compositions than for daily wear. Finally, while developing skills in character makeup, special effects and professional event visuals may also require realistic, contemporary, or dramatic looks.

Good makeup artists are paid very well. If you are not taught makeup design in your college classes, you should take master classes in makeup artistry.

CHAPTER 3

ENVIRONMENTAL CONSCIOUSNESS: ECO-FRIENDLY AND SUSTAINABLE FASHIONS

"Cheap fashion is really far from that, it may be cheap in terms of the financial cost, but very expensive when it comes to the environment and the cost of human life."

– Sass Brown

SOCIAL MEDIA AND TREND SHOPPING

Skills to Know: *Economics, Psychology, Consumer Behavior, Marketing*

Influencers have a significant say in market demand. Social media icons with hundreds of thousands of followers engage readers in discussing brand quality, price, sustainability, accountability, new designs, and fair treatment of employees. Studying these systems in college offers the chance to gain a global view of past and present trends.

Consumer behavior drives investment. This infusion of money, in turn, spurs on technology development like in-app purchases and integrated augmented reality, allowing potential purchasers to try on items and test out products. Seamless online shopping experiences encourage purchasing, while artificial intelligence highlights items for customers by preference choices. As a result, there is significant potential for industry growth.

SUSTAINABLE, RECYCLABLE, AND REUSABLE

Skills to Know: *Environmental Science, Sustainability, Design*

The greater global consciousness surrounding eco-friendly consumer products caught the fashion industry by storm, accelerating in 2022 with concepts like vegan leather, mushroom leather, slow fashion, ethical manufacturing, and second-hand clothing. Organic fabrics appeal to an individual's values. As an alternative to quick purchase wear and fast fashion, 'ethical' garments, like Eileen Fisher, hold a brand allure as people look for ways to protect the environment, protect workers, and ensure inclusivity. Stella McCartney's materials include recycled and natural fabrics.

Another trend in consumer purchasing is recycling and sustainability tags. Students may want to research and investigate the implementation of environmentally sound sales before an admissions or job interview, if the college or company offers one.

Cheaply made, fast fashion puts the planet at risk with its polymer-derived microplastics, synthetic fibers, and chemically-infused fabrics. When clothing is washed or heated, chemicals and plastics enter our water lines and damage our ecosystem. Thus, the term "sustainable" is not synonymous with clean or fresh, but tantamount to materials made with natural fibers and non-toxic fabrics throughout the material production and garment lifecycle. Recycling has also become increasingly popular.

Lightly worn garments are the latest in a growing trend. While second-hand shops are growing online and in brick-and-mortar stores. Closed-loop recycling offers a sustainable option to reduce raw material extraction and production. Additionally, garment reuse decreases landfill waste. Thus, fashion designers must be increasingly creative in reimagining style and product development from previously crafted items. With the growing number of second-hand stores, shoppers have a wide selection of unique clothing items.

PRODUCT PASSPORTS

Skills to Know: *Economics, Business, Human Resources, Social Issues*

Fashion companies are rolling out RFID chips and product labeling to let purchasers know the brand sustainability quotient, raw materials used, commitment to employees (diversity, healthcare, fair wages), and corporate standards. Customer's desire to know more has also driven companies to be transparent online regarding their corporate practices. On the business side, brands will be better able to determine product authenticity, prevent counterfeiting, and create an environment of loyalty, consciousness, and trustworthiness.

This escalating trend includes digital IDs like QR codes, NFC embedded tags, and RFID chips as well as non-digital biodegradable labels. Sustainability labeling offers an awareness and accountability tool, providing information about the fabric – authenticity, water usage, carbon footprint, location/date where the garment was produced, employer treatment, supply chain, the longevity of wear, even identifying the flock of sheep where the wool was shorn and its vaccinations. These traceable identifiers are not yet uniformly formatted, but, one day, they are likely to have universal requirements like food labels.

B CORP CERTIFICATION

The B Corp model is to re-imagine this century's commitment to sustainability. With the goal to generate profit while helping the planet, B Corps undergo a rigorous certification process, comprehensive assessment, and verification of social and environmental performance. B Corp Certification is a third-party evaluation on all stakeholders from the B Lab, "the nonprofit network transforming the global economy to benefit all people, communities, and the planet."[1]

---

1   B Lab, "About," *B Lab,* n.d., https://www.bcorporation.net/en-us/movement/about-b-lab

The definition of a B Corp:

> *Certified B Corporations are businesses that meet the highest standards of verified social and environmental performance, public transparency, and legal accountability to balance profit and purpose. B Corps are accelerating a global culture shift to redefine success in business and build a more inclusive and sustainable economy.*

The fashion industry's commitment to sustainability drove companies to seek ways they could be more eco-friendly and purposeful, while reducing global inequity. To generate and promote better business practices, companies and organizations banded to meet high standards of environmental consciousness and social accountability. B Corp fashion brands are given grades based on their commitment to ensuring an inclusive, sustainable economy.

Some companies like Cotopaxi donate a percentage of their revenue to end poverty and their employees commit a percentage of their paid work time volunteering in their community. Meanwhile, service-oriented companies, like Tentree, have an Earth-First commitment, planting ten trees for every purchase. Tentree makes choices "where the planet and its people come first, always. Tentree's goal is to reach 1 billion trees by 2030."[2] Similarly, companies like Allbirds, Patagonia, Frank and Oak, Bombas, and United By Blue commit to environmental sensitivity.

---

2   Tentree, "About," *Tentree,* n.d., https://www.tentree.com/pages/about

PROFILE: PATAGONIA[3]

Patagonia's Mission Statement: We're In Business To Save Our Home Planet.

Our Reason For Being
At Patagonia, we appreciate that all life on earth is under threat of extinction. We aim to use the resources we have—our business, our investments, our voice and our imaginations—to do something about it.

Build The Best Product
Our criteria for the best product rests on function, repairability, and, foremost, durability. Among the most direct ways we can limit ecological impacts is with goods that last for generations or can be recycled so the materials in them remain in use. Making the best product matters for saving the planet.

Cause No Unnecessary Harm
We know that our business activity—from lighting stores to dyeing shirts—is part of the problem. We work steadily to change our business practices and share what we've learned. But we recognise that this is not enough. We seek not only to do less harm, but more good.

Use Business To Protect Nature
The challenges we face as a society require leadership. Once we identify a problem, we act. We embrace risk and act to protect and restore the stability, integrity and beauty of the web of life.

Not Bound By Convention
Our success—and much of the fun—lies in developing new ways to do things.

---

3 Patagonia, "Our Mission," *Patagonia,* n.d., https://www.patagonia.com.au/pages/our-mission

CARBON FOOTPRINT AND ENVIRONMENTAL SUSTAINABILITY

The United Nations called on the fashion industry to lessen its environmental impact, promote sustainable consumption, reach its Sustainable Development Goals, follow the UN Framework Convention on Climate Change, and commit to the Paris Climate Agreement. As the need for sustainability becomes more urgent, innovation, digitization, reuse, pollution, and logistics will be the key topics of conversation. Industry leaders have called for eco-conscience transparency with the goal of a net-zero environmental impact.

The apparel industry is one of the biggest polluters on the planet. Textile mills generate one-fifth of the world's industrial water pollution and use 20,000 chemicals, many of them carcinogenic, to make clothes. Chinese textile factories alone produce about three billion tons of soot—air pollution linked to respiratory and heart disease—every year by burning coal for energy. Most of the world's textile factories are in developing countries where governments cannot keep pace with the industry's massive pollution footprint.[4]

The textile industry
1. produces global greenhouse gas emissions from the incineration of clothing
2. manufactures garments made with microplastics
3. leaves untreated toxic pollution
4. creates wastelands of landfills
5. transports tons of clothing in damaging supply chain operations
6. is responsible for harmful chemicals in dyes, pesticides, and detergents

Container ships filled with fashion industry garments travel from low-labor-cost countries like Bangladesh, China, India, Indonesia, and the Philippines to first-world countries every day. At the end of the life cycle, waste appears in countries willing to accept vessels containing fast-fashion discards. "The global fashion industry produces over 92 million tonnes of waste per year. In the U.S. alone, over 17 million tons of used textile waste are generated annually." For example, 39,000 tons of discarded clothing fill Chile's desert. Furthermore, a quarter of global CO_2 emissions come from the transportation industry, which is projected to double by 2050 with e-commerce leading the way.

---

4   NDRC, "Encourage Textile Manufacturers to Reduce Pollution," *NDRC*, n.d., https://www.nrdc.org/issues/encourage-textile-manufacturers-reduce-pollution

As the fashion industry's carbon footprint expands, environmental sustainability practices are even more important. Circular use of garments from growth to decay needs to begin with raw material production. Textile producers need to lead the way encouraged by fashion brands.

THE FUTURE OF THE FASHION INDUSTRY

Tornados whipped through the fashion and beauty industry as companies were swept into mergers, acquisitions, and partnerships. With small companies rising and medium-sized companies whisked into the winds of change, environmental consciousness rises to the top of the wind tunnel. In the swirl to offer consumers 'ethical' wardrobes, some companies are in a race to find new eco-friendly threads and fabric while also pointing themselves toward artificial intelligence and augmented reality to convey their message.

NATURAL TEXTILE FIBRES

COTTON   **LINEN**   **BAMBOO**

HEMP   **WOOL**   **SILK**

SYNTHETIC TEXTILE FIBRES

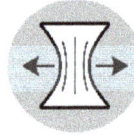  

ELASTANE   **ARAMID**   **NYLON**

 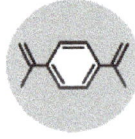 

ACRYLIC   **POLYESTER**   **PU LEATHER**

THE RACE FOR BIO-DEGRADABLE TEXTILES

Many synthetic textile fibers are not biodegradable and could take more than a century to decompose. This situation caused brands to hunt for new fibers as consumers ask how much of an environmental impact is the clothing going to cost in the long run from farming and processing to production and shipping. Fabrics made from cotton, silk, and hemp are household names, but you might be surprised at fashions made from apples, pineapple, and cork.

Sustainable Jungle offers this list of sustainable fabrics.

Sustainable Natural and Vegan Fabrics

Bamboo Linen	Organic Cotton	Recycled Cotton
Cork	Organic Hemp	
Organic Bamboo	Organic Linen	

Vegan, Synthetic Fabrics

Econyl	Recycled Polyester

Sustainable Semi-Synthetic Fabrics (mostly vegan)

Apple Leather	Lyocell	Scoby Leather
Bamboo Lyocell	Modal	S.Cafe
Brewed Protein	Pinatex	Woocoo
Cupro	QMilk	
EcoVero	Qmonos	

Animal Derived Natural Fabrics (sustainable depending on source)

Alpaca Wool	Down	Silk
Camel	Merino Wool	Vegetable Tanned Leather
Cashmere	Sheep Wool	Yak Wool

Fashion designers will be on the cutting edge of creating the next wave of sustainable textiles. Meanwhile, fashion merchandisers will be hard at work articulating and marketing eco-friendly products to this environmentally conscious generation. This moment in history can be defined by a dramatic transformation in the way we live, the way we work, and the clothing we choose to wear.

"There is no beauty in the finest cloth if it makes hunger and unhappiness"

– Mahatma Gandhi

CHAPTER 4

COSTUMING FOR SHOWS AND THEATRE: DESIGN FOR DRAMATIC MOMENTS

"All the world's a stage."

– William Shakespeare

A theatre, hushed just before the curtains open, is magical. Patrons who sense that magnificent enchantment, discover a transformative, goosebump-eliciting experience, reminding them that anything is possible. Even a river can be turned into chocolate as Willy Wonka and Charlie Bucket discovered in their search for inner peace and happiness in *Charlie and the Chocolate Factory.* Similarly, Dorothy took a yellow-brick road to discover new friends and braved a menacing forest filled with winged monkeys to discover that her family loved her dearly in *The Wizard of Oz.* Willy, Charlie, Dorothy, and every other character in drama, musical theater, and films come alive through the imaginations of costume designers.

Stories transform concepts and imaginings to writing and from scripts to dramatic re-enactment. Those who eat the cake in *Alice in Wonderland* grow to new heights drinking in the magnificence of the theatre. Simply standing on a pitch-black stage with rows upon rows of empty chairs is a remarkable experience. The stage is a metaphor for life as everyone lives on a stage, performing in their own play. It's humbling.

Shakespeare provided his own commentary.

> "All the world's a stage,
> and all the men and women merely players:
> they have their exits and their entrances;
> and one man in his time plays many parts ..."

—*As You Like It,* Act II, Scene 7, 139–142

Behind the curtain, a different kind of magic happens. Costumes create mood and ambiance, depicting grand moments like the balcony scene in *Romeo and Juliet* depicting societal barriers that can thwart love. The riverboat, *Cotton Blossom*, in Jerome Kern and Oscar Hammerstein's musical comedy *Show Boat*, provides a floating palace addressing the social issues of racism and inequality. As the show begins and the curtain rises, excitement builds, witnessing each character's garments, accessories, and makeup.

Iconic sets like the chandelier in *Phantom of the Opera*, dramatic moments like the helicopter scene in *Miss Saigon*, and a carnivorous, human-eating plant in *Little Shop of Horrors* bring theatre to spectacular glory. Audience members experience the dynamic sight and sound display.

Meanwhile, costume designers enchant audiences, Superwoman dons an indelible red, white, and blue outfit, accessorized with a gold belt, and Dorothy dazzles the Munchkins with her spectacular ruby red slippers. Identifiable masks like the iconic masterpiece designed by Maria Björnson and worn by the Phantom in *Phantom of the Opera* or the outfits designed by Paul Tazewell and showcased by the *Hamilton* cast stand out in our memories.

If you pursue your goal to become a costume designer, you will enjoy an exciting career. Have fun using your creative talents, and live each moment fully, developing invaluable skills that are transferable to other jobs you might choose. As you transition, remember that life is a journey, not a destination. Theatre is a thrill ride of grand proportions.

Knowing how to sew and design could lead you into fashion design should you decide to change your career. If you can create sets and have carpentry skills, you can build creative spaces in a home or office. Even Halloween sets and costumes can be remarkably fun to produce.

To work in theatre or film, you will find that most professionals with full-time positions have Bachelor of Fine Arts (BFA) or Master of Fine Arts (MFA) degrees in theatre arts. You can earn this degree focused specifically on costume design or technical theatre or a more general degree in theatre arts. Either way, you are set with the general skills. Before, during, and after your educational foundation, you just need experience.

The journey you are taking will have its ups and downs, but you will have stories to tell for the rest of your life. Enjoy this magical experience.

IMAGINE DOROTHY'S RUBY RED SLIPPERS OR GLINDA'S FAIRY TALE GOWN AND WAND

Design is pure creativity, right? Not exactly. Certainly, ingenuity and innovative idea generation are a must. However, when it comes to theatre, considerably more goes into the thinking process. Costume designers must thoroughly conceptualize and internalize the story's big picture. Ultimately, they must envision and execute how they would tell the tale in pictures.

Seven Cs of Costume Design

1. Creative
2. Clear
3. Concise
4. Compact
5. Communication
6. Collaboration
7. Complete

Creativity is fundamental. Afterward, the story's visual imagery needs to be told clearly so that people can see the story and internalize the mood, meaning, purpose, time period, socioeconomic climate, and emotion. The elements of a story are folded into one or more sets of visual pieces – moving parts in a jigsaw puzzle that, alone, says little, but together illuminates the entire picture.

At the same time, the show is not long. The limited timeframe necessitates brevity and conciseness. While plays, musicals, films, and commercials can range in duration, each has a beginning, middle, and end. Films, plays, and musical theatre must complete the entire thought with all components fitting together.

The stage or scene is compact in space. All of the action needs to happen within the frame of the stage or a lens. Yet, these components are confined to spatial limitations within the given area. While theatrical stages range in size, film locations can be much larger. Nevertheless, there are still bounds on action scenes that can take place on set. Every image, costume, or set piece needed to tell the story must be within the borders.

Shows do not take place in a vacuum. They are visualized and constructed as a team. Not only must the costume designers know the story and understand the context, but they must also communicate effectively with the director at the start. From the very beginning, there should be a clear line of communication.

Collaboration is essential. The designer may propose a couple of ideas, though they must be conceptualized with the director's leadership. Consultation with other cast and crew members is also necessary, including the technical director, production manager, scenic charge artist, prop master, costume designers, and other team leaders. By talking through opportunities for improvement, pitfalls in design elements, and financial and spatial limitations, the team can efficiently and effectively produce the synergy to craft the best representation of the story.

In the end, the story must be complete. Whatever needed to be communicated must have its rise and fall. The costumes and sets must reflect the perspective, conflict, climax, resolution, and overall theme.

Theatres are alive, buzzing with activity. Although the pandemic presented challenges to in-person plays and musicals, films continued to be created and theaters returned to enthusiastic audiences. Omicron's December 2021 last-minute heartbreaking shutdown disappointed thousands, though the song "No Day But Today", in the musical *Rent* reminds us,

There's only us,
There's only this,
forget regret,
or life is yours to miss.
No other road,
no other way,
No day but today.

Historically, theatres have always bounced back, even in the most catastrophic times. Shows and styles may change; budgets may tighten; designs may reflect the momentary mood.

While few alive today will ever forget the impact the pandemic had on life, liberty, and disparity, people will remember that "somewhere over the rainbow, bluebirds fly." We, too, will fly again, as will theatre. Unfortunately, the saddest moments will not completely disappear.

Theatres took a huge hit, stopping production teams. Theatre will come back stronger as will those who brought energy and life to the stage. Costumes will be created and stitchers will resume their roles. Feverish tech crews will construct sets, create props, paint miniature villages, and move tons of material. We will all move on.

CHAPTER 5

RETAIL AND E-COMMERCE: INDUSTRY KNOWLEDGE, TECHNOLOGY SKILLS, AND SOCIAL MEDIA

"I think it is really important to have a sense of business. As a designer you can get so wrapped up in the design and fashion side that you forget the business side."

– Tommy Hilfiger

FASHION DESIGN AND MERCHANDISING

Fashion designers envision, create, and produce, while fashion merchandisers consider markets, evaluate data, plan campaigns, and promote sales. While fashion designers must look ahead to future tastes, trends, and needs, fashion merchandisers must make decisions about the apparel line for a specific season, evaluate demand, select appropriate amounts, and manage sales. For the fashion designer, graphic arts, stitching, photography, and presentation are central to the work. However, for the fashion merchandiser, accounting, marketing, and statistical skills are essential. Visual displays, advertising, and sales comprise one component of fashion marketing, while the other involves the apparel creation, supply chain, distribution analysis, and business of the products sold.

Fashion designers begin the process by looking ahead, considering what consumers want, and designing their unique style. Meanwhile, fashion merchandisers must predict the future. Prognostications are aided by using past sales data, economic projections, global events, and experience with the fashion cycle. Fashion merchandisers must often plan four seasons ahead to forecast what trendy items people will want in the following year. This process requires envisioning volumes, products, styles, locations, and price points.

After meeting with designers and laying out the merchandise they plan to sell, the wheels go into motion with construction, manufacturing, distribution, showcasing, and sales. Errors in forecasting can be devastating. Thus, fashion merchandisers must rebound from miscalculations and career-altering rollercoaster-like turns.

Resilience is an essential skill with retail's decline and the rise of online sales. E-commerce has experienced a significant market share increase. The "Forrester 2021 Online U.S. Retail Forecast" predicts that brick-and-mortar sales will rebound to take 71% of the retail sales by 2024, though changes are likely to take place.[1]

Fashion groups, like Only The Brave (OTB) saw significant success, surpassing pre-pandemic levels with brands like Amiri, Brave Kid, Diesel, Maison Margiela, Marni, Jil Sander, and Viktor & Rolf. LVMH, with 150,000 employees and brands like Louis Vuitton, Christian Dior, Fendi, Givenchy, Bulgari, Marc Jacobs, Tiffany & Co, Chaumet, and TAG Heuer also showed significant growth. Meanwhile, fashion

---

weeks are gaining renewed excitement with those in New York, London, Paris, Milan, Frankfurt, Copenhagen, Rome, Ukraine, Sweden, New Zealand, Spain, China, Bulgaria, USA, and Costa Rica. January and February continue to be big months for fashion. The Miami Swim Week is also significant along with the bonanza of fashion events in late summer and early fall.

QUALITY, VALUE, AND PRICE

Understanding the consumer is the first step to success in this nearly $1.9 trillion industry. In the United States alone, sales of apparel, footwear, and accessories are expected to reach $500 billion. Who is buying? One-third of all sales are from Asia, while Europe commands the second-highest spot for apparel purchases. Additionally, the types of clothing demanded vary from country to country. Thus, studying consumer behavior and quantitative analysis of target personas is essential.

When people vacation, celebrate, or go out, they tend to wear fun or luxury clothing. However, when families are hunkered down, they tend to be more casual and relaxed. Likewise, when people feel like they can spend money freely, they do not mind purchasing high-quality items, even when they are more expensive. Yet, when money is tight, individuals tend to spend much less. Furthermore, demand, like the post-pandemic increase in activewear purchases, drives customers to find the kinds of items they desire. Thus, personal income and lifestyle increase consumer demand.

Knowing the industry and company demographics is essential, as is studying statistics. Coresight Research released a report stating that in 2021, retailers would suffer the consequences of the continued pandemic with 10,000 store closures for a 14% increase from 2020.[2] The losers were the luxury and high fashion stores. Meanwhile, grocery, dollar stores, and sports apparel markets survived tumultuous market adaptations. In part, this resulted from the impact of the remote workforce and fluctuations in workforce availability. Individual companies rode out the waves of highs and lows.

At the same time, numerous questions arose. What socioeconomic groups tend to buy from a specific brand? How can quality, value, or price entice these individuals? What can clothiers do when faced with supply chain bottlenecks? Without ordered products appearing in stores during the appropriate season, consumers may take their purchases elsewhere, brand reputations may become tarnished, and companies may suffer.

The answers to these questions are complex, but the key is to reach the consumer. The problems that occurred during the pandemic are some of the reasons why Farfetch, Lyst, Depop, Holition, and Intelistyle popped up into the market raising millions of dollars and offering sales and merchandising options for fashion designers to connect with retailers and individual customers.

This industry segment is huge with the valuation of Farfetch at over $1 billion. Meanwhile, Lyst allows customers to follow their favorite brands, Depop offers a marketplace that has more than 10 million users, Holition allows brands to adopt 3D technology and AI sales interfaces, and Intelistyle syncs outfits with a customer's physical body. These and other innovations have upended the marketplace and inspired numerous fashion designers and fashion marketers to rethink how they envision and invent fashion's future.

Meanwhile, boutique stores cannot compete with the prices large companies charge since they buy in volume. However, they can be very successful in more localized communities with one-of-a-kind items that large retailers do not sell. Thus, education in fashion design and fashion merchandising is more than just knowing what people like but how to locate target customers

---

2   Coresight Research, "US and UK Store Closures Review 2020 and US Outlook 2021," Coresight Research, January 28, 2021, https://coresight.com/research/us-and-uk-store-closures-review-2020-and-us-outlook-2021/.

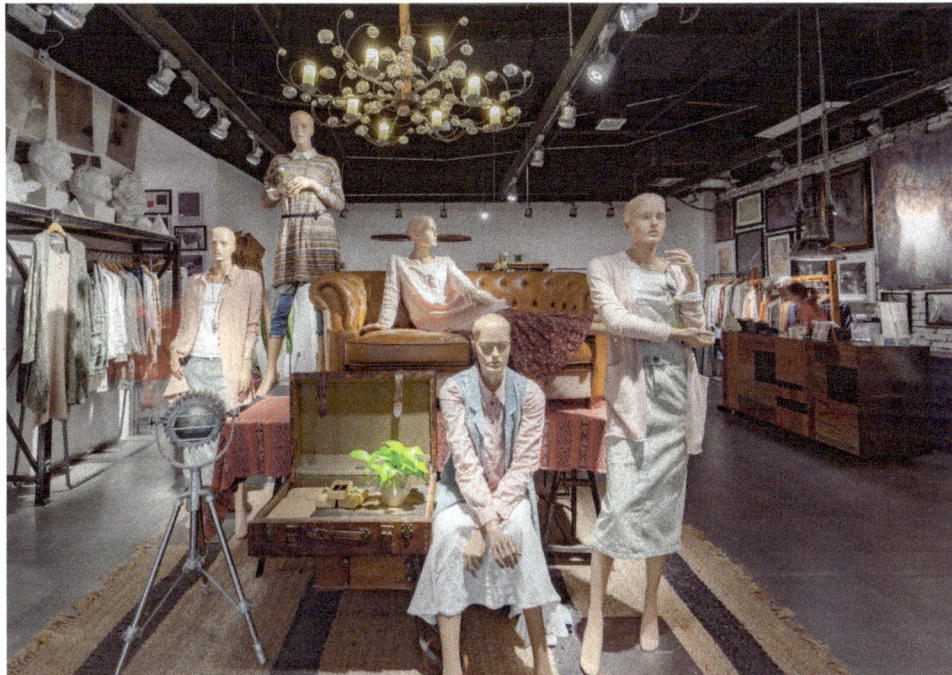

BRAND COMPETITION

Individuals typically migrate to the same brands time after time because they know what they will get, and they like how they feel in those clothes. So, how does the fashion merchandiser get a customer's attention to try a different brand and maybe attract them to their apparel? What drives a purchaser online or to an outlet store if they traditionally purchase from a luxury brand storeroom. You will learn this in college. Suffice it to say that with nearly 100,000 apparel stores in the United States, the landscape of fashion brands is highly competitive.

In the United States, the fifty largest companies hold approximately 70% of the market share. Breaking into this space is tough. Success depends upon merchandising, advertising, and marketing. The goal is for companies to effectively capitalize on their target market. Customer service is essential.

According to Brand Finance, the top 50 fashion brands in 2021 are:

1. Nike (USA)
2. Gucci (Italy)
3. Louis Vuitton (France)
4. Adidas (Germany)
5. Chanel (France)
6. Zara (Spain)
7. Uniqlo (Japan)
8. H&M (Sweden)
9. Cartier (France)
10. Hermes (France)

11. Rolex (Switzerland)
12. Dior (France)
13. Tiffany & Co. (USA)
14. Chow Tai Fook (China)
15. COACH (USA)
16. The North Face (USA)
17. Anta (China)
18. Victoria's Secret (USA)
19. Omega (Switzerland)
20. Puma (Germany)
21. Burberry (Great Britain)
22. Ralph Lauren (USA)
23. Ray-Ban (Italy)
24. Levi's (USA)
25. Lululemon (Canada)
26. Prada (Italy)
27. Bulgari (Italy)
28. Old Navy (USA)
29. Under Armour (USA)
30. Moncler (Italy)
31. Michael Kors (USA)
32. Yves Saint Laurent (France)
33. Fila (South Korea)
34. Next (United Kingdom)
35. Primark/Penneys (Ireland)
36. Tommy Hilfiger (USA)
37. Pandora (Danish)
38. Calvin Klein (USA)
39. Armani (Italy)
40. Givenchy (France)
41. Lao Feng Xiang (China)
42. Skechers (USA)
43. TAG Heuer (Switzerland)
44. New Balance (USA)
45. Valentino (Italy)
46. Hugo Boss (Germany)
47. Converse (USA)
48. Timberland (USA)
49. Loewe (Spain)
50. Bosideng (China)

By knowing the industry and using data-informed decision-making, fashion designers and fashion merchandisers serve customers by providing them with what they demand in a way that serves the public and the company. The education, training, and work experiences serve as a foundation for a rewarding career.

CHANGES IN THE RETAIL FASHION LANDSCAPE

During the pandemic, retail stores could no longer pay rent, and customers no longer came in droves to retail stores. As a result, underperforming stores shuttered, pivoting corporate focuses out of enclosed malls and onto the web. With two Christmas seasons down and very little foot traffic, fashion merchandisers had to rethink the marketplace and find new avenues to make their mark.

Demand changed too. With fewer people going to offices, office wear, like suits, ties, and professional women's wear, lost traction in exchange for work-from-home comfort clothing, sportswear, and smart clothing. Fashion designers and fashion merchandisers need to be able to see trends, like the casualization of apparel. Smart casual, leisurewear, even in the office, a trend that began before the pandemic, is now prevalent across industries and corporate offices as people slowly returned to workplaces.

Even the design of retail stores will need to change due to consumer demand for quick purchases with less exposure to other customers, fueled by concerns about risk, fear, and uncertainties, and short tempers of people who have little patience. Convenience shopping is the new mantra, along with touch-free curbside pick-ups. Marketers will need to reassess how to encourage shoppers to buy that one extra item they did not know they needed if they are not physically going into a store.

CYBERSECURITY

Skills to Know: *Website Development, Online Banking, Accounting, Reputation Management*

As virtual companies spring up and online forums grow, cybercriminals have used this opportunity to invade, terrorize, and demand ransoms. Cybercrime keeps people up at night. By invading a website, cybercriminals can encrypt files on a victim's computer, locking down the site, and demanding a ransom.

Internet and computer fraud includes using the internet to execute a vindictive, malicious, or illegal attack on another computer to obtain data, damage software, or disable its functions in order to obtain a financial gain. Cybercrime is somewhat different in that the reasons are not always money but could be for personal, political, social, environmental, or whimsical reasons.

Challenges to companies – large and small – include

- Cyber Extortion – demand for your money, belongings, or information
- Data Breach - stealing proprietary/brand information
- E-Mail Spoofing – a spamming technique to trick users into thinking a message came from an individual or company
- Forgery - reproducing a signature or copy of a document, banknote, or work of art
- Hacking – By digitally entering your computer, criminals can access your camera and watch, hear, and spy on you and your conversations
- Harassment – bullying, ruining your reputation, or revealing personal information
- Identity Theft - identity use to impersonate, harass, or conduct a crime

- Information Piracy - breaking into customer accounts
- Intellectual Property Attack – Your proprietary information, recipes, formulas, codes, and methods can be stolen, sold, and reused
- Phishing - tapping on a link for a great deal
- Predators – nefarious individuals who prey on the vulnerable for sex, drugs, or money
- Stalking – individuals who watch your actions online or in-person for a nefarious reason

Cybercrime is inconvenient, frustrating, and costly. It can ruin your reputation, deplete your bank accounts, bankrupt a company, and harm your family, friends, or employees. Altogether, cybercrime wreaks havoc in victim's lives. Fixing the problem after the fact, unlocking the computer, and repairing brand damage is significantly harder and more costly than protecting a site before the crime occurs.

Our digital world leaves open the doors to voyeurs and criminals who can access your information with new and more sophisticated resources. Criminals will always exist, but you can be more aware, key accounts, protect yourself, manage your privacy, report cybercrime, and prevent extensive damage by responding quickly with expanded knowledge.

DIGITAL FASHION'S GLOBAL VILLAGE

In 2005, when Thomas Friedman published his book, The World Is Flat, people took greater notice of the changing world dynamics. Employees could be easily hired who live on the other side of the planet, designers could bring their ideas to life outside of offices, and products could be manufactured, printed, or enhanced outside of production houses. The fashion industry took notice too. More garments, footwear, and eyewear than ever before began to be constructed thousands of miles away.

Supply chains redefined their models and projections, relying on new standards and logistics for trucks, trains, planes, and shipping. The fashion industry's marketing strategies needed to be retrofitted to a new paradigm of creation, production, and delivery. Along with the planning and processes, investment poured into 3-D worlds where glamour and style reigned.

Creatively inspired social media outreach was developed, reaching millions, along with glistening shopping mall showrooms in the metaverse. The first deliveries to popular 3-D digital retail centers will produce revolutionary changes to digital fashion's global village. As the engines fire up to energize these changes, trustworthy customer relationships must be built and communications must transmit both luxury and value.

As you head to college, you will enter a whole new world that does not yet exist but is terribly exciting. Ride the wave into the future with your grace and style.

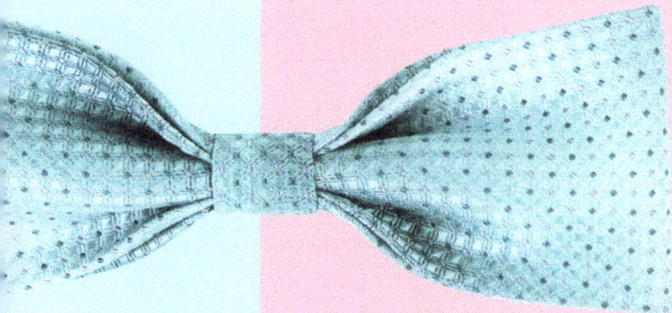

CREATE
YOUR
BRAND

CHAPTER 6

GAINING EXPERIENCE: INTERNSHIPS FOR HIGH SCHOOL, COLLEGE, AND BEYOND

"The whole purpose of education is to turn mirrors into windows."

– Sydney J. Harris

UNLOCK THE DOOR: STEP INSIDE

Internships are the key to unlocking the fashion industry's door. Enter! The exciting next step through the door of opportunity is the beginning of your remarkable career. Awaiting you on the other side is a thrilling adventure. Don't let the modern interior spaces and beautiful décor catch you off-guard, the swirling wind of activity inside a 100-mph storm.

Get off to a good start by being organized. Start looking long before you want to begin. Just like college applications are submitted six to ten months ahead of time, you should also begin planning ahead of time. If you are considering a summer internship, you should start searching during your Christmas break. Applications frequently open at the beginning of the new year for summer internships, and the deadlines close earlier than you may expect. Create a digital or hard copy calendar system that works for you with dates, deadlines, contacts, interviews, and networking opportunities.

Note that internships may be posted at your school or on websites and social media locations. You will not be the only one poised to jump in and get a head start. Companies soon become inundated with requests for more information, applications, and follow-up calls. If you know of someone in the organization to whom you can send your information first or who could follow up on your behalf, contact them, explaining that you are interested in a summer internship.

USE YOUR COLLEGE EXPERIENCE TO OPEN DOORS

College can be challenging, rigorous, and exhilarating. While there are tons of projects and opportunities, you need to choose. Do not squander all of your time. Instead, use some of it to find an internship. If you have a project in a fashion design class to interview someone, choose an industry professional and make a connection. Connect with people in the industry – NETWORK while in college. Get some experience. Any experience is a start. You can build on whatever step you take. Your first moments in the fast-paced fashion industry may be tough, scary, and challenging, but take advantage of the opportunity anyway.

SKILLS

You are now on the hunt to locate the doors you want to open and the keys to unlock the door. While internships are difficult to obtain, you need to have the required skills. Build these ahead of time. Look through job descriptions of the fashion positions you want and take classes in these areas or study the technical, website, or social media skills ahead of time. Then, when you are writing your resume and cover letter, include each of the abilities you can contribute to the position.

Writing skills are valuable. You can start gaining traction and developing your writing skills by publishing your own fashion blog or one for a company. You might want to try fashion journalism for a style magazine writing articles and submitting pictures.

COMPETITION

There are more than fifty people for every one position – even the unpaid internships. The fashion industry is competitive. Some hopeful interns have networked, helped out industry workers, offered free designs, edited articles, and carried out significant tasks. These actions happened long before they walked through the glamorous doors. Many potential interns are willing to do extra tasks to find that magical key.

Merely sending in a resume will not get you very far. You need to show initiative. Passively sending a resume and cover letter does not show much drive or desire. No matter what skills you have, persistence, determination, commitment, desire, and hunger are essential in the fashion industry. Your resume and cover letter are very likely to evaporate into the ether if you send it into cyberspace.

Also, do not apply to only one internship unless you know the person who is choosing the intern, and you are guaranteed a position. There could be hundreds of applicants. If you are determined to get an internship, apply to a few. The process can be arduous but worth the effort.

REFERENCES AND CHECKS

In the final rounds, companies will check your references and may call the people you chose to refer you. Follow up with your recommenders. Make sure you back up your resume experiences regarding club membership, education, and certificates. Finally, look over your social media accounts, even those you do not list on your resume or cover letter. The companies are likely to look up your Instagram, Twitter, Facebook, YouTube, Vimeo, Pinterest, etc. Make sure that you have touched all bases regarding images, text, appropriateness, responses, etc.

RESUMES AND COVER LETTERS

Many people use resume and cover letter templates. The benefit is speed and a sense of going in the right direction. However, these tend to be generic, even if your substance is unique. If you cannot format the resume as you like it, you might create one from scratch, have someone help you create the resume, or go into your career center to have an expert give you some guidance. Either way, your job is to stand out and not look like every other applicant.

Neither your resume nor your cover letter should be more than one page. Few busy people will ever look at the second page. If a page is placed on a desk, they rarely turn the page over or flip to other pages. Thus, for your resume, your job is to clearly and neatly display your background on one page. Make sure that you include any experience in the fashion industry, including retail, design, journalism, or photography. If you took related classes or participated in fashion clubs, include these. For your cover letter, make sure you read the job description and include the relevant skills you have along with evidence that you understand that specific company.

JOB APPLICATIONS

Read the application announcement carefully. Follow the instructions. If they do not want a resume, do not include one. If they want a photograph, make sure you provide the image in the format they want. If they want a sample of your art, designs, or writing, deliver the type and amount as specified. There are almost always instructions. For example, attachments may have viruses, so these may need to be sent via another format like WeTransfer or DropBox. Read these notations first so that your application does not get thrown out from the start. Also, make sure to write the subject line of any e-mail as specified. Otherwise, the e-mail may be automatically deleted or sent to spam.

INTERVIEWS

The company will need to discover what you are like to work with in person. Even if some work is remote, personality can shine through in-person and virtual interviews. The image you present provides the company an essential first look as to what you might look and act like in their offices. As you prepare, keep the company's corporate culture in mind – trendy, streetwear, business casual, suits, dresses, boots, all black, all white, or all pink.

Search the brand. Look at images online of what their employees look like in stores, offices, or tradeshows. If you wear your favorite cashmere sweater or a St. John suit, the look may be inappropriate for the company's fashion ensemble image.

You may have an individual interview, a group interview, or one that is online and asynchronous. In the last type, the company will send you a link to questions, and you will record and return your video answers.

JOB RESPONSIBILITIES

That depends. Every internship is different. During your first internship, you may be offered opportunities to sit in on meetings, provide suggestions, and contribute to big decisions. Each responsibility you are given is a step in the right direction. You will review, edit, design, write, produce content, manage tasks, and do whatever is required to quicken the delivery of the next project. The pace of work can often be likened to a tornado of duties – demanding, exhausting, and thrilling at the same time.

Work ethic is essential. Certain expectations come with the territory – come early, leave late, do extra work, and provide value. Without delivering these extra benefits to the company, you will find it difficult to get the good reference you will need to open the next bigger door. After all, your value begins when you relieve your supervisor's stress, complete all of the tasks, and also produce income.

SALARY

Most internships are unpaid. Unless you have previous experience specifically in the fashion industry, you are a trainee. You have much to learn. Consider your first internship as a training program since you are literally learning how to work independently. Your value begins when you produce income for the company. In the beginning, the tempo, day-to-day responsibilities, and unspoken expectations can be stressful. Your first position in the fashion industry offers a frame of reference – a first step into a fast-paced and glamorous world.

Once you have your first internship, your second internship will allow you to take a few more steps forward. If this second internship is unpaid, you need to make the experience valuable to learn new skills, take on more responsibility, gain more independence, and network. However, there are also paid internships. Depending upon your experience, skillset, and focus, paid internships can range from minimum wage to $30 per hour.

INTERNSHIP OPPORTUNITIES

One basic but most direct way to find an internship is on a company's website. These postings include the jobs, requirements, and applications. There is no fee and little concern that your information will be sold to other companies. The open jobs are listed. There is clarity about positions that are outdated or closed. Contact information is provided as well as the detailed job descriptions and skills necessary. Why apply for a position in which you are not qualified or will not be considered?

Many other sites have fees, keep your data, sell your information, or force you to click on outside links. However, many people use external websites for their search. Here are a few job listing options:

- Ed2010.com – Fashion Journalism
- FindSpark.com
- Indeed.com
- Internship.com
- InternQueen.com
- InternMatch.com

Below you will find another internship opportunity. More internships are posted on our website. Note: we do not ask for or receive a fee for these. We just post internships we find.

Nordstrom – The Ambassador Program @ Nordstrom: Define the Future of Retail

https://www.nordstrom.com/browse/theambassadorprogram
theambassadorprogram@nordstrom.com

This internship offers high school and college students (ages 14-22) with the opportunity to share ideas and experiences while gaining mentorship in digital styling, content creation, merchandising, marketing, social media, design, technology, and retail industry business. Students will explore career interests and get advice. While this is an unpaid internship, college scholarships are available. You do not need to live near a Nordstrom, but there is a 30-minute application.

FINAL NOTE

Some students often feel they have no chance given the number of applicants and only a few openings. Competition does exist in the fashion industry. Many applicants have significant experience. Often, very talented applicants are turned down in favor of an individual who has an inside connection. Connections are often made through a college career center or a professor who knows people in the industry. Nevertheless, someone will get a position. You could be that person.

Everyone wants to work for the same major brands. However, few look for up-and-coming creators, startup companies, or smaller establishments. While you may have your heart set on your dream brand, starting small may give you valuable learning experiences. Starting at the bottom of the ladder is not a bad place. With discipline, diligence, and training, you will climb the ladder to where you envision your life.

CHAPTER 7

WHAT IS THE DIFFERENCE BETWEEN AN AA, AS, BA, BS, BFA, AND MFA?

"A man paints with his brains and not with his hands."

– Michelangelo

UNDERGRADUATE AND GRADUATE DEGREES

AA – Associate of Arts – a 2-year degree

AS – Associate of Science – a 2-year degree

BA – Bachelor of Arts – a 4-year degree

BS – Bachelor of Science – a 4-year degree

BFA – Bachelor of Fine Arts – a 4-year degree with most classes focused on art

MFA – Master of Fine Arts – a 1-2-year degree earned after the BA, BS, or BFA

Basically, BA and BS degrees are degrees that typically offer a liberal arts foundation along with a major or concentration in a specific subject. Meanwhile, a BFA is considered a professional arts-focused degree with fewer courses in English, science, math, social science, and the humanities. Thus, the BFA is a specialist qualification in the arts. A BA or BS degree in fashion design or fashion merchandising is also valuable. The BFA is more focused on the specific area of art you choose.

The BA and BS degrees include significantly more liberal arts classes and thus are more general degrees. However, the intention of the BFA degree is for students to pursue an arts-focused curriculum, and thus there are fewer general subject courses.

Finally, while many AA or AS degrees are focused on providing technical or professional skills for fashion design, an AA or AS in these areas are often interchangeable. Similarly, a BA or BS in fashion design or fashion merchandising are also relatively interchangeable. However, a BFA may be seen as different since there is typically more coursework focused on your specific pursuit, and thus, you may have more technical experiences and knowledge than someone who has a BA or BS.

AA – ASSOCIATE OF ARTS

The Associate of Arts degree is typically a 2-year general studies degree offered online or in-person by a community college. However, some universities offer AA degrees as well. The Associate of Arts degree focused on liberal arts courses often has no barrier to entry, meaning that students can enter most AA programs with a high school diploma or the equivalent. Some students take a longer or shorter time to complete the AA based upon their skills upon entering the program, certainty about the direction they are heading, and the transfer requirements for the program they desire. For example, students majoring in business may have additional business, communication, accounting, and economics requirements and need to create an academic plan early in their program to finish in two years.

AS – ASSOCIATE OF SCIENCE

The Associate of Science degree is very similar to the AA. However, the AS degree frequently emphasizes science and math and often has additional requirements.

BA – BACHELOR OF ARTS

The Bachelor of Arts degree is typically a 4-year degree offered online or in-person by a college or university. However, a few community colleges offer BA degrees as well. Some students complete their BA in fewer years depending upon AP/IB credit, dual enrollment in high school, and summer/intersession classes. College programs have stricter or less stringent requirements depending upon the school. The Bachelor of Arts degree frequently requires students to take lower-division (first and second year) liberal arts courses before taking specialized courses focused around a major or concentration in their third and fourth years. Some students take a longer or shorter time to complete their BA based upon their skills upon entering the program, certainty about the direction they are heading, and their chosen major. According to the National Center for Educational Statistics, college advisors aid students in finishing "on time" though less than half of all students in the United States who start a BA program do not finish their degree in four years.[1]

BS – BACHELOR OF SCIENCE

The Bachelor of Science degree is very similar to the BA. However, the BS degree frequently emphasizes science and math and often has additional requirements.[2]

BFA – BACHELOR OF FINE ARTS

The Bachelor of Fine Arts is a 4-year college degree focusing on the arts. BFA students are often not required to take as many English, science, math, social

---

1   IEC NCES, "Digest of Education Statistics, Table 326.10," IES NCES, n.d., https://nces.ed.gov/programs/digest/d20/tables/dt20_326.10.asp?referer=raceindica.asp

2   Ibid.

science, and humanities courses. However, they must still complete roughly the same number of credits as a person who earns a BA or BS, and the courses are not necessarily easier. BFA students frequently take general art requirements to lay a foundation in drawing, graphic design, and courses in their specialty area during their first two years, along with basic writing and quantitative skill-building.

BFA students are traditionally art-in-practice students who learn the technical craft of their art form while putting in enormous numbers of hours practicing their skill doing assignments and participating in internships and experiential learning. Students who know that they want a future in the arts often finds this avenue perfectly tailored for their pursuits. However, students who change their minds and transfer to a university in another degree program may require an additional year to make up for coursework they have not completed.

MFA – MASTER OF FINE ARTS

The Master of Fine Arts is a graduate degree for students who have completed their BA, BS, or BFA. This degree takes one to two years depending upon the program, coursework, and experiential component, which may be a capstone, practicum, internship, or thesis. While there are also MA and MS degrees, many art students who continue to earn their master's degree in the arts chose to focus on their field of interest. The MFA is an intensive immersion into a higher level of skill-building. However, students who graduate with an MFA have a broader range of talents and experiences than those who earn their bachelor's degrees. While admission into these programs is generally selective, with planning, preparation, and a good portfolio, there are options for you to pursue your interests.

THE SEVEN MAJOR DIFFERENCES BETWEEN THE ASSOCIATE, BACHELORS, AND MASTER'S DEGREES

1. Starting Point
2. Academic Discipline
3. Time to Completion
4. Location of the Education
5. Educational Costs
6. Earning Power
7. Professional Opportunities

STARTING POINT

Most students who begin with an Associate of Arts (AA) or Associate of Science (AS) have no college credits. Starting from scratch with their college education, they accumulate their 60+ units beginning from this community college starting point. While most students earn AA or AS degrees at a community college, some earn this degree at a 4-year college or university.

The AA or AS is either a terminal degree, meaning that the student will not continue on with their bachelor's degree or just a steppingstone to their BA, BS, or BFA. The difference between the associate's and bachelor's degrees is just the starting point.

The starting point for students who pursue a bachelor's degree may be farther along the traditional 4-year pathway. Meanwhile, the starting point for the master's degree (MA, MS, or MFA) begins after obtaining a bachelor's degree.

ACADEMIC DISCIPLINE

Every degree encompasses different requirements. Requirements for the AA differ from an AS. Similarly, the requirements for the BA, BS, and BFA also differ. With two additional years of coursework, the BA, BS, and BFA are more thorough. The MA, MS, and MFA build upon the bachelor's degree and even deeper. Fashion design students will not take the same classes as fashion merchandising, though a few may overlap. Though both are behind-the-scenes players in the fashion industry, the essential skills for each career area are distinct; course requirements are also unique.

Furthermore, with the myriad of combinations, it is rare that any two undergraduate students have the same exact classes in the same exact order. Since the requirements for a chemistry degree are not the same as for biology and graphic design differs from fashion design or fashion merchandising, the various degrees not only include a different number of credits but different types of classes and program specifications.

TIME TO COMPLETION

Associate of Arts (AA) and Associate of Science (AS) degrees typically take two years, while most BA, BS, and BFA degrees are 4-year programs, depending upon full-time or part-time status. Students who transfer in credits or earn credits otherwise can reduce their time to completion.

Some students may choose to extend their education in fashion design or fashion merchandising by earning a second bachelor's degree in another field. By cross-training, students open more doors. For example, a degree in business on the bachelor's level or Master's in Business Administration (MBA) may lead to leadership positions.

Time in college can be reduced. Some students enter a BA, BS, or BFA program having already completed college credits because they were dual-enrolled or they took college classes directly through a college or university ahead of time. Some students have taken AP/IB tests from taking higher-level tests while in high school and earned qualifying scores to be granted credits by the college or university. Other ways students can enter at a different starting point are with credit-by-exam, CLEP tests, experiential credits, and those granted in the military.

Colleges and universities are keenly aware of the challenges students face today with work, illness, and family responsibilities. Thus, many schools of higher education offer flexible enrollment with opportunities for part-time, evening, weekend, and online classes.

LOCATION OF THE EDUCATION

The AA and AS are earned at colleges that grant 2-year degrees. The location may be at a local community college or a university. BA, BS, and BFA programs are offered at a 4-year college or university. However, with online classes, students have the flexibility to take classes from colleges farther away as well. Thus, the location in which a typical student studies is not as set as it once was. Nevertheless, the in-person internships are often situated in corporate hubs and thus require grounding to a specific location.

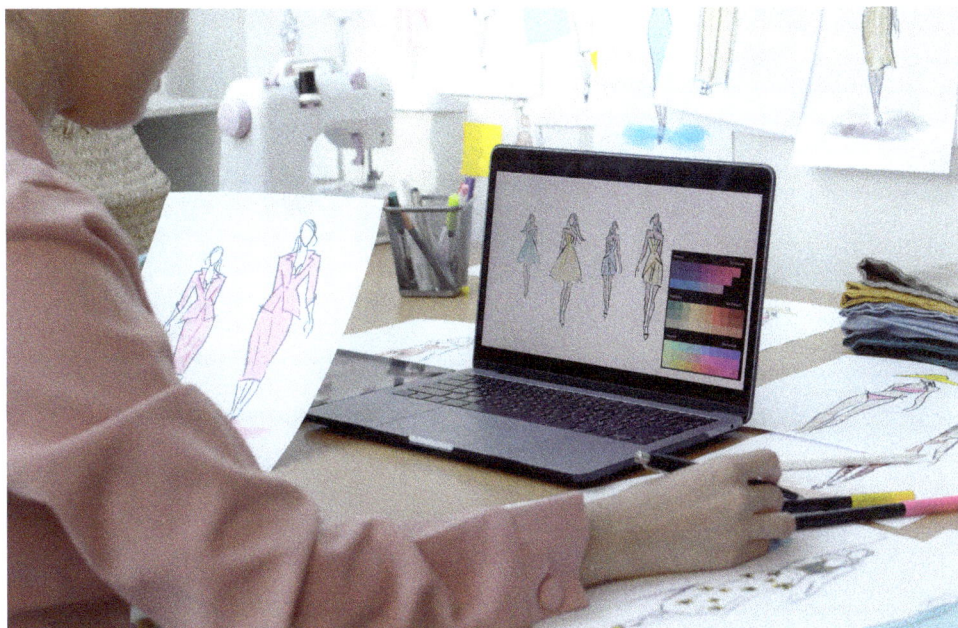

EDUCATIONAL COSTS

Since the AA or AS requires a shorter amount of time and is typically completed at a lower-cost community college, the cost for an associate's degree is typically less than a bachelor's degree. Master's degree programs cost more per credit but take less time than a bachelor's degree.

On the other hand, many students can obtain financial aid in the form of grants, loans, and both merit and need-based scholarships. This aid can pay for school and reduce debt after college.

EARNING POWER

Students with more education can earn more. According to the 2019 National Center for Educational Statistics (NCES) data for the median person,[3]

---

3   IES NCES, "Annual Earnings by Educational Attainment," IEC NCES, May 2021, https://nces.ed.gov/programs/coe/indicator/cba

Master's Degree or Higher - $70,000

Bachelor's Degree - $55,700

Associate's Degree - $43,300

High School - $35,000

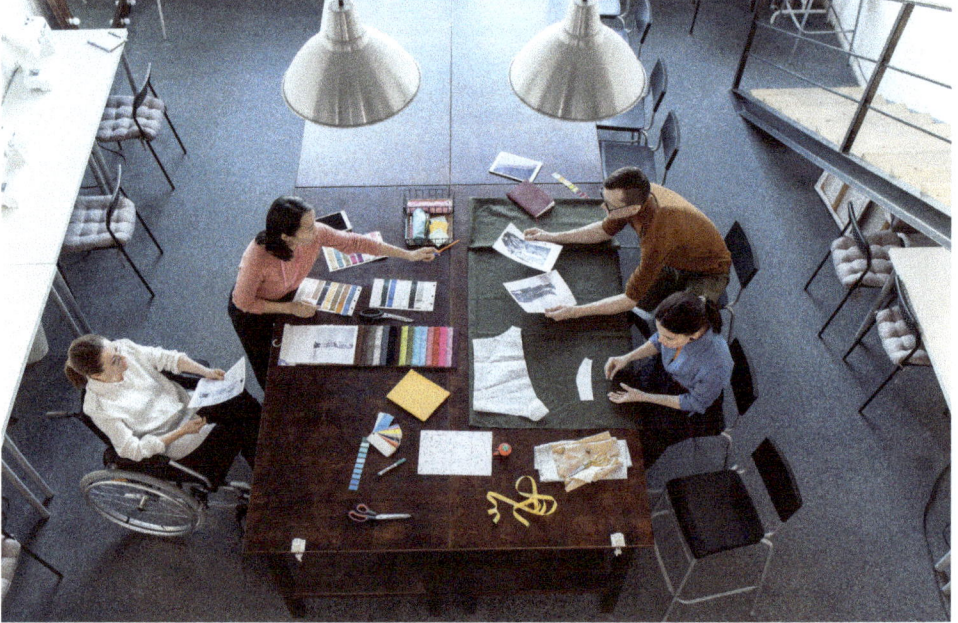

PROFESSIONAL OPPORTUNITIES

Earning a BA, BS, or BFA opens more doors than an AA or AS. Similarly, an MA, MS, or MFA opens more doors than a BA, BS, or BFA. Companies typically seek employees with greater knowledge and professional experience. However, the caveat is that some companies do not want to pay more for individuals with more education but less experience. Training takes up much of a company's budget. There are numerous technical, software, and communication skills required when entering the professional arena. A nimble fashion designer or fashion merchandiser contributes most when they have soft skills, like creativity, collaboration, and self-motivation.

Nevertheless, the retail industry has the dual challenge of needing the manpower to design, distribute, and market apparel while also keeping the budget down so that they can afford to continue producing trending fashions. While colleges promote and develop skills and competencies, internships help cut down the learning curve when entering a position. This is best done by hiring those graduates who already have experience. Thus, a student with a BFA sometimes has more experience than one with a BA or BS, though plenty of students with BA and BS degrees built a portfolio of knowledge by starting early. Also, they may have a broader liberal arts sense to understand the economics, social conditions, statistical data, and psychology of changing attitudes toward fashion.

CHAPTER 8

UNIVERSITY OPTIONS: WHAT COLLEGE PROGRAMS ARE BEST FOR FASHION DESIGN?

"Working hard is important. But there is something that matters even more: Believing in yourself."

— **Harry Potter**

There are a myriad of choices of where to focus and what colleges will satisfy your goals in the fashion industry. If you love the creative artistry of clothing choices and accessorizing, you might find fashion design, styling, packaging, or advertising interesting. However, if you prefer the more problem-solving and analytical side of the industry, you might enjoy management or marketing. Although only 56 colleges are profiled in this book, there are many more colleges offering similar majors. As a place to start your search, this book includes primarily four-year undergraduate college programs that are popular choices with students, though there are a few with two-year and a few graduate programs.

In choosing the right program to fit your interests, you want to explore the majors, courses offered, and requirements for admission. Every school is different. I also recommend applying to ten schools so that you have choices. The profiles for fashion design schools are provided in the back of this book, separated by region for your convenience. You might also want to know alumni who graduated from the schools, internships offered, and Special Opportunities to interact with people in the industry.

In the ever-changing world of standardized testing, determine which colleges require the SAT or ACT. This is likely to change from year to year depending upon availability, test disruptions, and college decisions.

The cost of your education may be a significant factor. You want to check the cost of attendance for each of the schools you are considering. However, do not let the price tag stop you from applying. First, rarely do people pay the full cost of their education. Second, more than half of all students qualify for financial aid. Third, almost all colleges offer merit scholarships. These are typically based upon talent, academics, and experience. If you have highly desired qualifications or a trifecta of skills, you may qualify for tens of thousands of dollars. Full-tuition scholarships are available as well. Many of the college's institutional scholarships are listed under the individual scholarship headings in the profile section.

Here are a few individuals in the fashion industry along with the colleges they attended.

Bernard Arnault – Chairman and CEO of LVMH, Chairman of Christian Dior SE
College: Ecole Polytechnique, France's leading engineering school

Francesca Bellettini – CEO YSL
College: Bocconi University, Milan and University of Chicago (study abroad)

Tory Burch – Ameican Fashion Designer
College: University of Pennsylvania in Art History

Maueen Chiquet – former CEO Chanel
College: Yale University – BA literature with an emphasis in film

Jimmy Choo (Datuk Chow) – Malaysian Fashion Shoe Designer based in the UK
College: Cordwainer's College, London (London College of Fashion)

Thomas Carlyle Ford – American Fashion Designer
College: Bard College at Simon's Rock, New York University in Art History
Parsons School of Design in Architecture

Daniel Del Core – German-Italian Fashion Designer
College: Istituto Europeo di Design Milan

Mossimo Giannulli – American Fashion Designer
College: Did not graduate from college

Isabelle Guichot – CEO SMCP – Board Member SMCP and Chargeurs
College: Hec Paris EESC (world-class business school)

Daphne Guinness – British Fashion Designer
College: Did not graduate from college

Alexandre Herchcovitch – Brazilian Fashion Designer
College: Santa Marcelina College in Fashion

Tommy Hilfiger – American Fashion Designer
College: Did not graduate from college

Kenneth Ize – Nigerian-Austrian Fashion Designer
College: University of Applied Arts, Vienna

Marc Jacobs – American Fashion Designer
College: Parsons School of Design

Betsey Johnson – American Fashion Designer

College: Syracuse University

Donna Karan – American Fashion Designer (DKNY)
College: Parsons School of Design

Nicholas Kirkwood – British Footwear Fashion Designer
College: Cordwainer's College, London - (London College of Fashion)

Stella McCartney – British Fashion Designer
College: Central Saint Martins (University of the Arts London)

Alexander McQueen - British Fashion Designer
College: Central Saint Martins (University of the Arts London)
Newham College (East Ham Campus)

Sandy Powell – British Costume Designer (3 Academy Awards; 15 nominations)
College: Central School of Art and Design in Theater Design

Miuccia Prada – Italian Fashion Designer
College: University of Milan, Ph.D. Political Science

Paula Schneider – CEO American Apparel
College: California State University, Chico in Secondary Teaching

Maisie Schloss – American Fashion Designer of Maisie Wilen
College: Parsons School of Design

Kate Spade – American Fashion Designer
College: University of Kansas, Arizona State University in Journalism

Sharen Jester Turney – Former President and CEO of Victoria's Secret
College: University of Oklahoma, B.A. in Business Education

John Varvatos – American Fashion Designer
College: Fashion Institute of Technology
University of Michigan, Eastern Michigan University

Charles de Vilmorin – French Fashion Designer
College: School of the Parisian Couture Union
French Fashion Institute

Kanye West – American Fashion Designer
College: American Academy of Art College, Chicago State University

TOP FASHION SCHOOLS IN THE U.S.

1. Fashion Institute of Technology, NY
2. Savannah College of Art & Design, GA
3. Parsons School of Design, NY
4. Fashion Institute of Design & Merchandising, CA
5. Pratt Institute, NY
6. Drexel University, PA
7. Rhode Island School of Design, RI
8. Kent State University, OH
9. Cornell University, NY
10. Academy of Art University, CA
11. Iowa State University, IA
12. Marist College, NY
13. North Carolina State University, NC
14. Colorado State University, CO
15. Otis College of Art & Design, CA
16. Auburn University, AL
17. University of Minnesota, MN
18. Thomas Jefferson University, PA
19. University of Delaware, DE
20. University of Texas, Austin, TX
21. Baylor University, TX
22. School of the Art Institute of Chicago, IL
23. LIM College, NY
24. University of North Texas, TX
25. University of North Carolina at Greensboro, NC

CHAPTER 9

COLLEGE ADMISSIONS, COURSEWORK, SKILLS, AND SCHOLARSHIPS

"The primary purpose of going to colleege isn't to get a great job. The primary purpose of college is to build a strong mind, which leads to greater self-awareness, capability, fulfillment, and service opportunities, which, incidentally, should lead to a better job"

– Sean Covey

With notable alumni like Michael Kors, Norma Kamali, Ralph Rucci, and David Chu as well as top professors and courses, some consider FIT to be the leading fashion design school in the country. Fashion Institute of Technology offers the following fashion design and merchandising degrees:

- BFA in Advertising and Digital Design
- AAS and BS in Advertising and Marketing Communication
- AAS in Communication Design
- BS in Cosmetics and Fragrance Marketing
- MPS in Cosmetics and Fragrance Marketing and Management
- BFA in Fabric Styling
- MA in Fashion and Textile Studies: History, Theory, Museum Practice
- BS in Fashion Business Management
- AAS, BFA, and MFA in Fashion Design
- AAS and BFA in Footwear and Accessories Design
- MPS in Global Fashion Management
- BS in International Trade and Marketing for the Fashion Industries
- AAS in Jewelry Design
- AAS in Menswear
- BFA in Packaging Design
- AAS and BS in Production Management
- BS in Production Management: Fashion and Related Industries
- BS in Technical Design
- BFA in Textile Development and Marketing
- AAS and BFA in Textile/Surface Design
- BFA Visual Presentation and Exhibition Design

Coursework includes classes like the following sample:

Fashion Management Course Options	Fashion Design Course Options
Sustainability in Fashion Merchandising	20th Century Style for the 21st Century Aesthetic
Corporate Social Responsibility	CAD for Fashion Design and Development
Data Insights and Fashion Analytics	Advanced Digital Fashion Design
Leadership Development for Retailing	Accessories that have Changed Fashion
Global Merchandising	Haute Couture Embellishments
Merchandising Strategies	Designer Sportswear Incubator

SCHOLARSHIPS

Nearly every school in the United States offers need-based scholarships. However, most schools offer merit scholarships. Many are listed in the profile section. Check it out.

Below are a couple of schools chosen at random to give you a sense of a few of the options listed in the profile section.

Marist College

- BFA in Fashion Merchandising

The Silver Needle Runway is the largest of Marist College's events, held since 1984. Continually growing, this student-produced showcase highlights student designers and their works, with approximately 2000 people in attendance. A presentation of awards and scholarships follows the runway show. Awards have been provided by Kate Spade, MPorium, Cutty Sark, and Young Menswear Association, among others.

Columbia College Chicago

- BA in Fashion Studies, BFA in Fashion Design

Applicants, including international students, are automatically considered for talent-based scholarships. A digital portfolio or audition is required. Numerous awards are offered.

Iowa State University

- BS in Apparel, Merchandising, & Design,

Iowa State offers merit-based awards to students of any major. These awards are based on GPA and ACT/SAT.

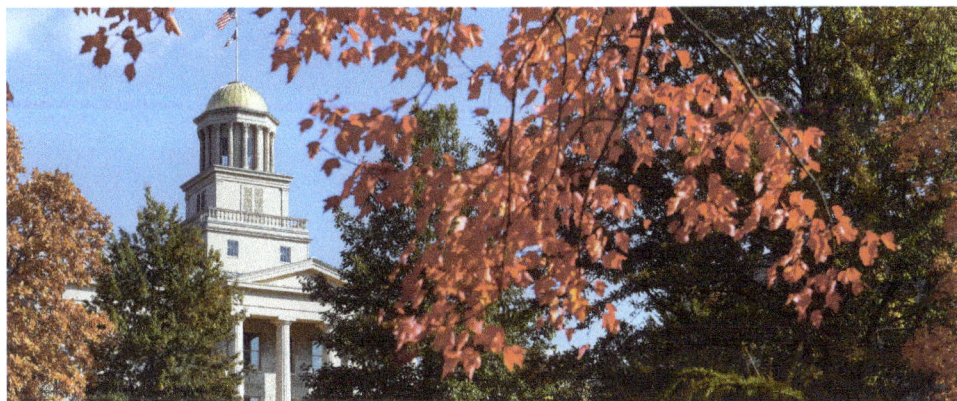

Savannah College of Art and Design (SCAD)

- BFA Fashion, BFA Accessory Design, BFA Jewelry, BFA Fibers

SCAD also offers two full-tuition scholarships: The May and Paul Poetter Scholarship and the Frances Larkin McCommon Scholarship. These two scholarships are based on superior academic and/or artistic achievement.

The Fields Family Prestige Scholarship and Jacques Weber International Scholarship offer fashion and textile students varying award amounts.

Otis College of Art and Design

- BFA in Fashion Design

Otis College Scholarships are awarded to students based on need, academic merit, and artistic merit. Otis Named Scholarships are awarded by donors such as Nike or Sony for students who maintain a 3.0+ GPA and typically require a recommendation from your department chair. Otis College also recommends students apply for outside scholarships. For more information, visit: https://www.otis.edu/financial-aid/scholarships

COLLEGE ADMISSIONS:

Success in the Face of Uncertainty

There are no guarantees in college admissions. However, planning is essential for success. The most beneficial advice is to pursue your passions with gusto, train to be the best you can be, take advantage of internships and experiences, and meet lots of people along the way. Remember, "life is a journey, not a destination." Often the journey is more exciting, leading to lessons, friendships, and indelible moments. However, the fact is…in the end, if college is your goal, then you need to know a few action items to remember for success.

Should you worry about grades? Of course. You should also take classes that will challenge you. Colleges pick the best candidates from those who apply. Students must be academically prepared, socially conscious, and talented in a few different areas in which they are passionate (conceptual design, graphic arts, costumes, theater, acting, singing, dance, musical instruments, debate, public speaking, leadership, athletics, community service, computer coding, robotics, construction, etc.).

This selection process is not that much different than companies picking employees. While colleges are more or less competitive, companies may have only one job and fifty resumes. Discover the unique drive and internal motivations within you that make you the very best you can be. Be exceptional at what you choose to do academically, personally, and professionally.

Most of all,

You Do You

TALENT FOCUSED

Not all schools require high grades and test scores. Many are simply interested in selecting students who are the most talented, most driven, and the most willing to be team players on the college campus. Thus, while you should take a solid set of courses and fulfill requirements, only the top schools emphasize completing a challenging curriculum, high grades, and standardized test scores.

FOR HIGHLY SELECTIVE COLLEGES, TALENT IS JUST THE BEGINNING

A few highly selective colleges seek extraordinary talent over academics, but most zero in on a student's challenging courses and high grades. To gain admission into the most highly selective colleges, you must take the most challenging course load you can manage and succeed. Highly selective colleges want disciplined scholars AND remarkably talented students.

Determine what you can handle, knowing that some colleges with extremely competitive admission will only take students who have completed more than ten AP, IB, or honors classes over the four years, including AP Calculus. AP Statistics is not of equal rigor in their eyes. Why, then, would these most competitive colleges require a class that is beyond the scope of what you need for your major? This situation is the $50,000 question. However, if this seems daunting, remember that most colleges accepting students for artistic fields do not need these types of classes.

College admissions can feel like a rollercoaster of energy and emotion. Creating a portfolio of talent, training, and experience is just the beginning. Meanwhile, some colleges want to see standardized test scores which are aided by practice. Applications and essays may seem easy at first, but managing the various requirements and deadlines can be difficult. Therefore, this application period is a good time to get a calendar and organize your tasks.

STANDARDIZED TESTING

A few schools require testing. Check first. Many colleges are test optional. This means that you are not required to take the SAT or ACT. However, if you do have a good score, it may make all the difference in accepting you. College admissions offices are studying this topic and considering their future policies. Much of their concern began with cancelations worldwide due to the pandemic. Schools did not want to let students into their site who may be infected. In addition, social distancing limited the number of students who could take a test at a site at a time.

Yet, college admissions decisions were once centered around grades and test scores. The change has rattled admissions departments. Meanwhile, colleges proclaim that test-optional truly means that the test is not required, but evidence proves otherwise. Thus, many students are still taking the test and working around the hurdles amid all of the confusion. Competition continues to drive students to present evidence to show that they are worthy candidates.

In the end, colleges need to make a final decision between very good candidates. If one student has a high score, that student may have a higher likelihood of admission depending upon the admissions committee's decision-making process. Data show that students who submitted scores within the college's range or higher were accepted at a higher rate than those without a score. Some schools are test blind in that they say that they do not consider your scores. A few of these colleges still provide a place for you to input your scores, thus, they are not truly blind. Nevertheless, this decision is yours. If the school does not require an admissions test, then you can choose to take the test. If your academics are solid and you are willing to prepare, you should take the test.

APPLYING EARLY

Early Action (EA), Restricted Early Action (REA), and Early Decision (ED)

With low acceptance rates, the chance to get more scholarship money, and chaos surrounding the cancellations and changes in AP, IB, SAT, and ACT testing, students clamor to apply early to schools. In addition, applications to top schools increased during the pandemic, resulting in colleges making difficult admissions decisions in their quest to build a diverse, talented, and engaged class of students. Furthermore, students applying early have access to many more scholarship options. This confluence sent students in droves to apply early and this trend is likely to continue.

In Early Action (EA), Restricted Early Action (REA), and Early Decision (ED), students apply in late summer or early fall to college and generally find out around winter break, though some decisions come out earlier and a few arrive later. This advantage not only includes students the chance for more scholarship money in some cases but the benefit of finding out early reduces the tension of the long waiting period to find out about Regular Decision schools.

Early Action (EA) and Restricted Early Action (REA) are different. In restricted early action, a limitation is placed on either how many or what colleges you can apply to simultaneously. Many REA schools do not allow students to apply to other early action schools, though some will allow students to apply EA to public colleges. In addition, some schools like Georgetown will allow students to apply EA elsewhere but not apply to a binding Early Decision (ED) program where the student commits to attending if they are accepted. However, most EA schools do not have these restrictions, and some students apply to a handful of EA schools during the Admissions process.

Early Decision (ED) is a binding agreement between the student and college with signatures from the student's parents and the high school. Each of these parties acknowledges and agrees that, if granted admission, they will attend. There are incentives. Frequently, acceptance rates are higher with ED. Also, at some schools, a large percentage of their class is filled with students who profess their unequivocal love for their dream school. Students who know they have a top choice school, have the necessary admissions requirements, and are committed to accepting the binding agreement to attend, should apply ED.

COMMON APPLICATION, COALITION APPLICATION, OR COLLEGE-SPECIFIC APPLICATION

Every college's process is unique. However, there are a few commonalities. In 2022, approximately 900 colleges used the Common App; about 150 colleges used the Coalition Application. A few used both. The University of California system has its own application as do the California State Universities and the Texas schools. The Common App and Coalition App may be started early. In your junior year, consider getting a head start on reviewing what is required. The college-specific questions may change each year. However, the basic application is generally the same and can be created ahead of time. At the end of July, make a copy of everything you have completed just in case.

In August, most admissions applications are open and ready for you to dive into the college-specific questions. Some schools admit on a rolling basis. 'Rolling' means that periodically, after all of the materials are received, the admissions committee determines who they will accept, and they send the notification right away. Many students are accepted as early as August. The thrill of acceptance cannot be overstated.

Complete the application fully. Think carefully about optional sections. Typically, they offer you the chance to provide the school with just the right cherry on top of the ice cream sundae. If you have absolutely nothing to say, then leave it blank. There are often required essays on the main Common App and the supplemental applications for each school. Some include scholarship essays. Start early.

DECISIONS, DECISIONS: WAITING FOR A RESPONSE

The period between submitting your application and getting your results may not require a tremendous amount of work, but it does require patience and diligence. First, most schools will send you a link to a portal where you will check your results, though the most important reason for checking every couple of weeks is to ensure that they are not missing something or have not offered you the chance to apply for an extra scholarship. Check your portal regularly. Otherwise, read the correspondence that the school may send through your e-mail.

Waiting is difficult. This is a tough period because students want to know. However, on the portal, the college typically lists the date they will send out the results. You will find out soon.

CELEBRATING ACCEPTANCES AND DEALING WITH REJECTION

Acceptance is not guaranteed. The probabilities are low at the most highly selective schools. However, you just need to work to have what it takes and give this commitment all you have.

Fashion Design - Top 10 Most Competitive Schools by Admit Rate

1. Cornell University - 11%
2. Washington University in St. Louis - 16%
3. Rhode Island School of Design (RISD) - 27%
4. University of Texas, Austin - 32%
5. Delaware State University - 39%
6. Fashion Institute of Design and Merchandising (FIDM) - 39%
7. California State University, Long Beach (CSULB) - 42%
8. North Carolina State, Raleigh College of Design - 46%
9. Moore College of Art & Design - 50%
10. Marist College - 55%

When you find out the results, you will celebrate your acceptances. Congratulations! These go on your list of wins. Check your financial aid and scholarship package. Money is often an important factor in making your decision. Consider visiting the school. Many students apply by only looking at pictures and profiles on a website or book. There is nothing that replaces the actual visit. After all, you will be spending a few years there.

However, you may not be accepted everywhere you apply. The pandemic's uncertainty added more question marks to an already complicated set of admissions processes. The buzzword for the 2020s is resillience. It is never easy to be rejected. However, rejection happens, and you will survive this. Note that many colleges still accept applications in April, May, and June. Look up those colleges if you did not get accepted or if you want to see what other schools might be good options for you. You will be surprised to see the colleges on the list.

WAITLISTS: THE ART OF WAITING

Confirm immediately if you are given a waitlist spot and still want to attend. There is often a deadline, and you do not want to miss this. If you are no longer interested or have selected another school, go into the portal and turn down the offer. Someone else is bound to be thrilled by your anonymous gift.

Next, if you are highly interested, find the location on the portal or site designated by the college to update them on what you have done – accomplishments, awards, extra class, honors, art, shows, or films. You only want to add what they have not yet seen, but if you have taken the initiative to do something more than what you originally stated on the application, by all means, tell them. You could just wait for their decision, but you are better off being proactive and showing that you really want to be at their school.

Students do get off of the waitlists at most schools. Meanwhile, you will have to deposit somewhere else before the May 1st deadline. Stay hopeful. This next year will be a significant step along your journey. Relax!

DETERMINING FINANCIAL AID

You do not need to complete the FAFSA (Free Application for Federal Student Aid) or CSS Profile (College Scholarship Service) if you do not need aid. However, a handful of schools want to see one or both of these forms to obtain scholarships. Check now since there are deadlines.

If you completed the FAFSA (and CSS profile, if required), the financial aid package you receive would be viewable on your portal. The college will delineate the amounts you will receive for grants, loans, and work-study. Some students turn down work-study, but I caution against that. There are jobs on campus where you conduct research, work with a professor, work in the library, or assist an athletic team. Some of these jobs pay well, and you might have even done them as a volunteer.

If your financial situation changed since you applied, you may be able to renegotiate the amount they offered.

CHOOSING THE RIGHT SCHOOL FOR YOU

Once you have acceptances, you need to make a decision. With the turmoil of the pandemic, disruption in clubs, sports, and experiential activities, and serious family health concerns, access to some opportunities has been non-existent. Most training and practice have been virtual. Furthermore, few students have traveled to visit colleges due to the crisis. However, with college costs for four years around $300,000 at some schools, college is the most significant investment some families will ever make. Furthermore, student loans can saddle a student in debt for a decade or more.

Financial decisions are key. However, there are many variables in deciding which school to choose. Will I be able to afford my education? Will classes be online or in-person? Will I be able to continue my training? Will I get to visit the colleges first? Can I live through the repercussions of stressful decision-making? Should I defer my admissions and take a year off?

Once you make your decision, focus on your future. What is trending? What do people want? How can you deliver?

You've Got This!

CHAPTER 10

PORTFOLIOS: COLLEGE ADMISSIONS REQUIREMENTS FOR FASHION DESIGN

"Putting on a beautifully-designed suit elevates my spirit, extols my sense of self, and helps define me as a man to whom details matter."

– **Gay Talese**

PORTFOLIOS: REQUIREMENTS, ACCESS, AND PREPARATION

Fashion design begins with a mental image and a sketch, though many students today translate their vision using graphic design software. Most students work independently, creating designs and visualizing how they will look on an individual, mannequin, animal, or some other form. In homes, dorms, and studios, fashion designers hone their craft, gaining inspiration from magazines, online images, and art of all forms.

Students practice, train, learn new skills, and evolve with the ever-changing forces of fashion. New team members are invited to be part of the school's fashion-focused community after submitting a portfolio and/or participating in an interview. Some schools do not require students to demonstrate any previous experience, preferring to train students from scratch. However, top fashion design faculty want to ensure that their students have the basic knowledge before they begin.

Collaboration, sense of humor, disciplined work habits, willingness to exceed the call of duty, and a positive attitude are some of the essential ingredients to success in this field and in their studios. Also, most fashion design faculty members want to get to know you and your inspirations, learn about your training, and how your skills can contribute to group efforts. Admissions evaluators in fashion design are not ordinarily interested in training you from scratch just because you are curious about this field and like the idea of producing your own clothing line. However, when they accept you, they commit to working with you. On the other hand, you must be talented and committed to working with them as well. Completely committed.

College classes and positions in fashion design often require long hours – sometimes all-nighters. Furthermore, you must balance your fashion design artwork and craftsmanship with often challenging academics. Thus, you must still succeed in your classes while developing a line for a fashion show. Experience in high school or summer studio art classes lets the school know that you can handle the rigors of detailed artistry with the rigors of school, managing both successfully. This is also why the college wants you to submit recommendations, particularly from an art teacher who can vouch for your capabilities.

While some schools will not interview or require a portfolio. You should be prepared to have samples of your work in pictures, video, website, drawings, recommendations, and written format, like an essay about your personal journey.

PORTFOLIO REVIEW AND INTERVIEWS

Portfolio review days were often in person, though some final reviews have been digital for a decade. These review opportunities allowed students to get in-person or virtual feedback from college representatives who, in turn, got to meet potential students. Nevertheless, digital portfolios were practically the sole way students presented themselves during the pandemic. One good reason for in-person portfolio reviews was to let students experience the school. Thus, when portfolio review days were on college campuses, students had the chance to visit the school, tour the facilities, gain a sense of campus life, learn about the program from the inside, meet representatives of other programs, and visit the dormitories.

PANDEMIC CHANGES

Yet, the pandemic demanded changes. With students unable to travel and colleges unable to allow students to visit the facilities, fashion design departments adapted their portfolios and interviews. Although many colleges were reticent, a few colleges took steps to offer online meetings, invitations to classes, and even in-person interviews.

Still, with very few other choices, colleges moved their interview process online. Zoom, a platform that was virtually non-existent before the pandemic, rose in prominence as the pre-eminent method. As this new modus operandum took hold and more students, faculty, and admissions officers became comfortable, the rollout began.

Pre-screening with resumes, drawings, displays, designs, fashion photography, and websites was fairly common before the pandemic. Application portfolios allowed students to input specified elements to a portal, and colleges began the evaluation process.

COSTS AND FASHION DESIGN PROGRAM VIABILITY

Frankly, colleges considered cutting funding to fashion design programs. Why maintain studios and associated staff when there were no fashion shows, and students could not access the sewing equipment and studio facilities for nearly two years? With an uncertain future, the cost of recruiting students and securing spots in a program that may no longer exist was called into question. Student costs were also a significant factor in some of the decisions.

The precariousness of life, concerns about health, and parents whose careers were in jeopardy were significant factors in the changes that took place. Families worried. Hunkered down in lockdowns, mandates, vaccine requirements, and illness, colleges needed creative options. After all, where should creativity begin?

ACCESS AND EQUITY

The other major factor was the costs involved. Many families could not afford to travel. With the growing concern for access and equity, colleges worked harder to make the process fair for all applicants. The 2020 spotlight of BLM and issues surrounding diversity, racial and social inequity took center stage.

Colleges looked for new ways to level the playing field for all applicants. By holding interviews on Zoom, Skype, Google Hangouts, Microsoft Teams, or Adobe Connect, students just needed a computer and an Internet connection. Quarantined or locked down, they could meet virtually from their home, school, or convenient location.

With a location in which the student was comfortable and without the financial burden of travel for themselves and often parents, students had greater access. For many students of color, interviews were significant barriers to entry. Removing these barriers became a central priority along with letting students know that everyone would have the chance to audition, interview, or be reviewed if they passed the initial portfolio evaluation process. Opportunity and access became the mantra of admissions offices nationwide.

Colleges sought new ways of putting together a diverse class. Creatively and thoughtfully, the playing field slowly leveled. There is more to do regarding access and equity, but steps were taken to allow more students to be part of the process.

EXAMPLES OF COLLEGE PORTFOLIO REQUIREMENTS

Portfolio requirements vary from school to school. More information is provided in the profiles in the second half of the book. Not all schools have portfolios, and not all schools have interviews. However, for schools requiring a portfolio, components often include a resume, letters of recommendation, essays, sketches, and demonstrations of artistic style.

The following are a few examples to gain a glimpse into portfolio requirements.

Note: This snapshot does not provide the full specifications. Please see each college's website for detailed portfolio requirements.

Cornell University

Submit the following via SlideRoom
- 4 prompts, approximately 150 words each
- Maximum 15 examples of fashion illustration, clothing designed, and textile design projects
- Secondary work samples of ceramics, crafts, glasswork, and/or paintings

Fashion Institute of Technology

Submit the following via SlideRoom
- 250-word essay
- **Project 1:** Sportswear Coordinate (3-6 images) - Create a mood/ inspiration page for sportswear with a written explanation for how the design is inspired by the mood page.
- **Project 2:** Fashion Design Artwork (4-8 images) – Original fashion design artwork on figures you drew. Include scanned or digital photos of actual 2x2 fabric swatches and identify the fabric type.
- **Project 3:** Sewing Project (4-9 photographs) – 2-3 garments you have sewn with front and back views on a person or mannequin.

Marist College

Submit via SlideRoom
- Inspiration mood board
- 200-word essay
- Design mix and match separates for a collection
- Drawings of original garment designs
- Design collection of mix and match separates
- Fabrics and flat sketches showcasting your thinking
- Hand or digital drawings of original garment designs (not traced)

Parsons School of Design

Submit via SlideRoom
- 8-10 images
- Parsons Challenge
- Create new visual work inspired by a theme within a piece submitted in your portfolio.
- Support your intellectual process by writing a 500-word essay.
- You may submit 2 additional visual pieces to demonstrate this process.

Pratt Institute

Submit via SlideRoom

- 12-20 examples of your most recent work
- Include 3-5 drawings from observation
- Do not include work that uses the grid system or copies photos or other's work

Rhode Island School of Design (RISD)

Submit via SlideRoom

- 12-20 examples of your most recent work
- Include examples of drawing from direct observation
- Up to 3 works may be research/preparatory work
- Also, choose a paired concept and make a work based on the prompt.

Syracuse University

Submit via SlideRoom

- You may submit a traditional or alternative portfolio with a 2D or 3D exercise
- 12-20 examples of your most recent work
- Include fashion-related works
- 1 short answer (200 words) and 1 writing sample (500 words)

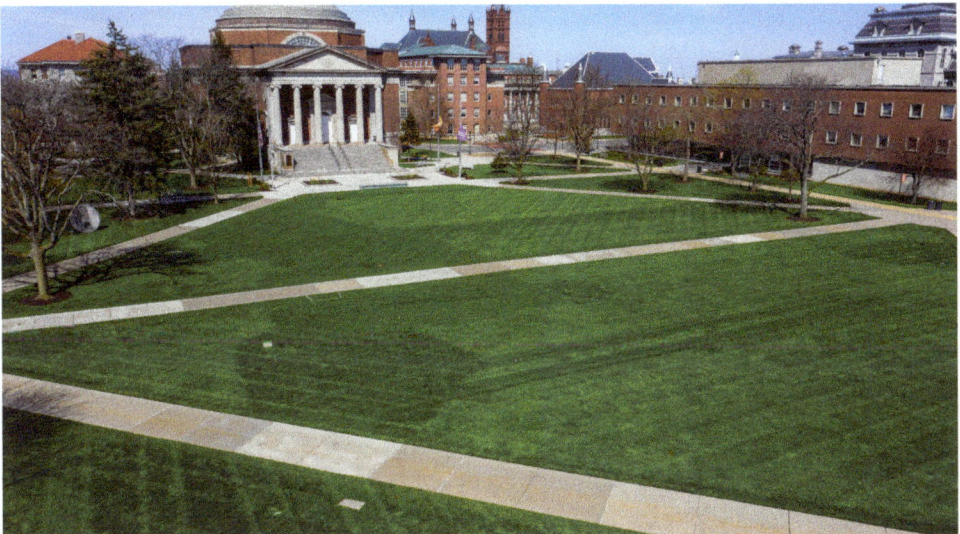

Follow the application and/or website instructions to submit your portfolio. Portfolios are submitted in a specific way for each college. Read each website to determine the college's particular requirements. Some use SlideRoom, while others use AcceptD or iFolio, and still others require preliminary materials to be submitted through the basic application or directly to the college.

SLIDEROOM

SlideRoom partnered with the CommonApp to integrate the portfolio into their admissions process. Not all schools use SlideRoom, but it is a popular platform. Students check a box on the supplemental form of the CommonApp, and a portfolio link appears. Colleges receive the application while also receiving the portfolio from SlideRoom when they import and view the student's data, and evaluate each based upon the college's requirements during that admissions cycle. Search features and image clarity make SlideRoom one of the most common platforms.

ACCEPTD

AcceptD is a popular platform for portfolios. Resumes, art, designs, essays, and other materials may be submitted. In-person interviews can also be scheduled through this site in one seamless process. Many colleges use AcceptD for its versatility.

IFOLIO

iFolio is a more recent addition to the college admissions scene. This modern digital platform offers an interactive portfolio. While iFolio is used more often for business interactions, interviews, and information sharing. Some colleges find this tool extremely beneficial.

YOU'VE GOT THIS!

Whatever format a college requires, students upload their materials to provide a more seamless process for colleges to evaluate students for their programs. The portfolio process may seem cumbersome, particularly if you are applying to five to ten colleges with four to five different methods of submission and four to five different sets of requirements. However, if you start early and are disciplined in the process, you can do it. Even if you start late, you can pull everything together. It's just a bit more stressful. Get started now and prepare for your future.

CHAPTER 11

COSTUME DESIGN: DEGREES AND REQUIREMENTS

"The only way to do our best work right now, is to work well together."

– Tim Carl

Costume design requires more than envisioning and drawing a costume. Costume designers must be skilled seamstresses and stitchers. Becoming an expert in sewing is a must. Most costume design programs are rigorous. Furthermore, pattern making requires mathematical skills as well as graphic design to layout and replicate patterns for various sizes. Costume design school will teach the workflow, production patterns, construction techniques, and finishing methodologies used in the industry.

Thus, the first three necessary skills are centered around creativity, drawing, and sewing. However, college degrees in costume design teach much more. Some of those skills include manually working with a life fit model, specialized cutting techniques with different kinds of scissors and hand stitching types for seams, hems, and crafting.

Costume design school will teach you skills for stage and film like breaking down characters from a script and conceptualizing their identities by developing a look book using mood boards, color stories, and illustrations. Creativity and ingenuity provide the fit within the historical period, theme, and emotional context. This entails stretching your mind by watching shows of all types and imagining what you would do to change the audience's feeling through the costuming.

Keep a small notebook with you to jot down inspiration as you witness it throughout your experiences.

At the beginning of the inspiration for this book, the plan was to only include profiles of the top twenty schools for costume design. However, every list seemed different, and everyone interviewed had a new college to add or a good reason why a school should be included. Thus, the profile section has approximately fifty schools. Nevertheless, there are some schools that traditionally rank in the top lists. Here is one of those lists.

According to the *Hollywood Reporter*, the top ten schools for Costume Design are:

1. California Institute of the Arts (CalArts)
2. Carnegie Mellon School of Drama
3. NYU Tisch School of the Arts
4. Savannah College of Art and Design (SCAD)
5. UCLA School of Theater, Film, and Television
6. The University of Missouri – Kansas City (UMKC)

7. Wimbledon College of Arts, University of the Arts London (UAL)
8. University of North Carolina School of the Arts (UNSCA)
9. USC School of Dramatic Arts
10. Yale School of Drama

FAMOUS COSTUME DESIGNERS

Edith Head: won 8 Academy Awards; 35 nominations
     College: BA University of California, Berkeley in French;
          MA Stanford University in Roman Languages

Milena Canonero: won 4 Academy Awards; 9 nominations
     Studied art, design history, and costume design in Genoa

Colleen Atwood: won 4 Academy Awards; 12 nominations
     College: Cornish College of the Arts in Painting

Irene Sharaff: won 5 Academy Awards; 15 nominations
     College: Parsons School of Design
               Art Students League of New York
               Académie de la Grande Chaumière in Paris

Charles Le Maire: won 3 Academy Awards; 13 nominations

Sandy Powell: won 3 Academy Awards; 15 nominations
     College: Central School of Art and Design in Theatre Design
Dorothy Jeakins: won 3 Academy Awards; 12 nominations

College: Otis College of Art and Design

Anthony Powell: won 3 Academy Awards; 6 nominations
College: Central School of Art and Design

TONY AWARD NOMINATED COSTUME DESIGNERS FOR A MUSICAL (2010 – 2020)

Greg Barnes for *Follies* (2012), *Kinky Boots* (2013), *Something Rotten!* (2015), *Tuck Everlasting* (2016), *Mean Girls* (2018)

Tim Chappel for *Priscilla, Queen of the Desert* (2011)

Linda Cho for *A Gentleman's Guide to Love and Murde*r (2014), *Anastasia* (2017)

Bob Crowley for *An American in Paris* (2015)

Marina Draghici for *Fela!* (2010)

Lizzy Gardiner for *Priscilla, Queen of the Desert* (2011)

Rob Howell for *Matilda the Musical* (2013)

Eiko Ishioka for *Spider-Man: Turn Off the Dark* (2012)

Michael Krass for *Hadestown* (2019)

Dominique Lemieux for *Pippin* (2013)

William Ivey Long for *Rogers and Hammerstein's Cinderella* (2013), *Bullets Over Broadway* (2014), *On the Twentieth Century* (2015), *Beetlejuice* (2019), *Tootsie* (2019)

Santo Loquasto for *Hello Dolly!* (2017)

Jeff Mahshie for *She Loves Me* (2016)

Bob Mackie for *The Cher Show* (2019)

Martin Pakledinaz for *Anything Goes* (2011), *Nice Work If You Can Get It* (2012)

Arianne Phillips for *Hedwig and the Angry Inch* (2014)

Clint Ramos for *Once on This Island* (2018)

Emily Rebholz for *Jagged Little Pill* (2020)

Ann Roth for *The Book of Mormon* (2011), *Shuffle Along* (2016), *Carousel* (2018),

ESosa for *Porgy and Bess* (2012)

Paul Tazewell for *Memphis* (2010), *Hamilton* (2016), *Ain't Too Proud* (2019)

Mark Thompson for *Tina* (2020)

Isabel Toledo for *After Midnight* (2014)

Matthew Wright for *La Cage aux Folles* (2010)

Paloma Young for *Natasha, Pierre & The Great Comet of 1812* (2017)

David Zinn for *SpongeBob SquarePants* (2018)

Catherine Zuber for *How to Succeed in Business Without Really Trying* (2011), *The King and I* (2015), *War Paint* (2017), *My Fair Lady* (2018), *Moulin Rouge!* (2020)

TONY AWARD NOMINATED COSTUME DESIGNERS FOR A PLAY
(2010 – 2020)

Dede Ayite for *Slave Play* (2020), *A Soldier's Play* (2020)

Bob Crowley for *The Audience* (2015), *The Inheritance* (2020)

Johnson Fensom for *Farinelli and the King* (2018)

Nicky Gillibrand for *Angels in America* (2018)

Soutra Gilmour for *Cyrano de Bergerac* (2013)

Jess Goldstein for *The Merchant of Venice* (2011)

Jane Greenwood for *Act One* (2014), *You Can't Take It with You* (2015), *Long Day's Journey into Night* (2016), Little Foxes (2017)

Desmond Heeley for *The Importance of Being Earnest* (2011)

Susan Hilferty for *Present Laughter* (2017)

Rob Howell for *The Ferryman* (2019)

Toni-Leslie James for *Jitney* (2017), *Bernhardt/Hamlet* (2019)

Michael Krass for *Machinal* (2014), *Noises Off* (2016)

Katrina Lindsay for *Harry Potter and the Cursed Child* (2018)

William Ivey Long for *Don't Dress for Dinner* (2012)

Christopher Oram for *Wolf Hall Parts One & Two* (2015)

Martin Pakledinaz for *Lend Me a Tenor* (2010)

Clint Ramos for *Eclipsed* (2016), *Torch Song* (2019), *The Rose Tattoo* (2020)

Constanza Romero for *Fences* (2010)

Ann Roth for *The Nance* (2013), *Three Tall Women* (2018), *The Iceman Cometh* (2018), *To Kill a Mockingbird* (2019), *Gary: A Sequel to Titus Andronicus* (2019)

Rita Ryack for *Casa Valentina* (2014)

Tom Scutt for *King Charles III* (2016)

Paul Tazewell for *A Streetcar Named Desire* (2012), *Hamilton* (2016), *Ain't Too Proud* (2019)

Mark Thompson for *La Bete* (2011), *One Man, Two Guvnors* (2012)

Jenny Tiramani for *Twelfth Night* (2014)

Albert Wolsky for *The Heiress* (2013)

Paloma Young for *Peter and the Starcatcher* (2012)

David Zinn for *In the Next Room (or The Vibrator Play)* (2010), *Airline Highway* (2015), *A Doll's House, Part 2* (2017)

Catherine Zuber for *The Royal Family* (2010), *Born Yesterday* (2011), *Golden Boy* (2013)

CHAPTER 12

POST-PANDEMIC EMPLOYMENT OUTLOOK: STATISTICS AND ECONOMIC PROJECTIONS

"Your dresses should be tight enough to show you're a woman and loose enough to show you're a lady."

– Edith Head

ECONOMIC OUTLOOK IN THE FASHION DESIGN AND FASHION MERCHANDISING INDUSTRIES

Fashion design attracts thousands of students each year to pursue a career in the creative side of fashion while fashion merchandising focuses on the business side of the industry, helping to improve a company's bottom line. There are numerous directions to go. Fashion merchandisers must have business skills and tend to make more money than fashion designers.

Even the fashion designer must understand the decision-making behind the marketer's coordination, organization, forecasts, display concept, sales, production, and distribution since one crucial mistake can cost millions. Positioning products for maximum customer visibility can be extraordinarily exhilarating. Fashion shows, creative styling, photography, videography, social media, and website visibility are attractive to the go-getter student.

The economic outlook for retail stores does not look good in the near term, but this will change with post-pandemic societal changes. For now, explore the e-commerce displays. What attracts you to these sites? Retail forecasters believe that retail will pick up. What are brick-and-mortar stores doing to get your business? Notice the changes in window displays, mannequins, styling, and sales racks.

Management requires attention to detail and attention to the needs and wants of its customers. Managers are paid better because they are held accountable for the success of stores. Consumer demands continue to change. Which companies are adapting well to these changes? If you find the business direction intriguing, take a few management classes along with your fashion design program. You will increase your versatility in the job market.

Whether you desire a more creative role or a more business-oriented focus, there is a place for you. However, there are typically more applicants than positions. With the volume of people choosing this direction, top jobs tend to go to those with more education and experience. Also, the more competitive markets will require additional skills, education, and ambition.

Do not let the number of people applying for undergraduate or graduate degree programs or an internship or a job stop you. If this is the field you want to pursue, pave the road in front of you and drive. An internship or two would not hurt you in your pursuit. Although most internships are unpaid, you will find that most applicants will have one or more.

If you are serious, you can make a fantastic career out of your pursuit.

Initiative-taking persistence, talent, creativity, and moxie can get you into your desired college program and career. You may have to start at the very bottom of the ladder, but you can climb the rungs methodically one by one.

Companies want to know the work ethic, personality, and professionalism of the employees they choose. An internship allows you to get to know their corporate climate better and allows them to get to know you better too. Thus, many companies hire the interns they feel are the best fit rather than choosing candidates from the piles of resumes and cover letters that have been submitted.

Education unlocks doors. In fashion design, this is also true. Graphic design, drawing, sewing, draping, stitching, and showmanship are invaluable tools in this career pursuit. Your education, highlighted on your resume, can move your application to the top of the pile.

FASHION DESIGN ECONOMIC OUTLOOK

Bureau of Labor Statistics - Fashion Designers

2020 Median Pay: $75,810 per year

Bachelor's Degree: Fashion Design or Fashion Merchandising

Number of Jobs in 2020: 27,800

Job Growth: No change

Location of Most Positions: New York and California

Fashion designers design and create clothing, accessories, and footwear. The work environment is predominantly in wholesale or manufacturing establishments, apparel companies, retailers, theater, dance companies, and design firms. The work is both creative on the design side and technical on the production side.

TECH DESIGNERS VS CREATIVE DESIGNERS

Do you like to sketch, illustrate, and do graphic design? You might love the creative design route. You will either draw on paper or use programs like Adobe Illustrator. You get to imagine and create fashionable garments. By choosing fabrics, adding trims and adornments, you will enhance whatever you envision.

Technical designers are less focused on inventing ideas and more honed in on apparel production. What instructions are necessary to create a particular garment? This detailed work includes providing clarity regarding patterns, notions, sewing, fit, and packaging. Technical designers are often called the engineers behind the garments. With fittings, alterations, and changes in the specifications, communication between the creative and technical teams is essential.

From concept (creative designer) to product specifications (technical designer) there are numerous steps to ensure that the garment makes sense.

Career Options Include:

Account Executive

Art Director

Beauty, Makeup, or Perfume Executive
Fashion Editor-in-Chief

Brand Manager

Consumer Behavior Analyst

Costume Designer

Creative Director

Design Director

E-Commerce Manager

Executive Retail Management

Fabric and Apparel Patternmakers

Fashion Analyst

Fashion Designer

Fashion Forecaster

Fashion Freelance Writer

Fashion Merchandiser

Fashion or Textile Buyer

Fashion Photographer

Fashion Publisher

Fashion Show Producer

Fashion Sustainability

Hand and Machine Sewers

Marketing Director

Marketing Manager

Pressers Textile

Product Developer

Product Lifestyle Manager

Public Relations Manager

Sourcing Manager

Stylist

Tailors, Dressmakers, and Custom Sewers

Textile Bleaching and Dyeing

Textile Knitting and Weaving

Textile Winding, Twisting, Drawing Machine Setters, Operators, and Tenders

Textile, Apparel, and Furnishing Workers

Whatever direction you pursue, if you lay a foundation, undaunted by the competition, and are unafraid of starting at the bottom, you will do fine. Hard work and creativity go a long way in this industry. Start by getting a solid education.

MANAGEMENT AND EMPLOYEE RETENTION

Skills to Know: *Management, Human Resources, Social Consciousness, Ethics*

One of the most significant challenges facing the years from 2022 - 2030 will be locating and retaining talent. The pandemic slowed education and learning with online classes, reduced access to faculty/advising, limited access to labs, inability to attend workshops, retail closures, and fewer conferences, meetings, and shows. Health concerns rose to the top of importance as did financial stress, job uncertainty, and social consciousness. Many students chose to work rather than study and start online stores when they could not access locations for community service or continue with their sport, instrument, or hobbies. With the changes in lifestyle and fears about health, safety, and wellness, many bright and talented students developed a fearless sense of autonomy and independence, while for others, the necessary skills ordinarily developed in school were fraught by limitations.

Finding talent within the changing hiring atmosphere will require new skills to retain staff. Employees are increasingly looking elsewhere for a better opportunity. This development will require managers to earn and harness employee trust and loyalty. Top brands use the appeal of their fashions to attract new talent to their companies. However, with numerous startups and entrepreneurial thinkers eager to define their own brand, many potential job seekers are not on the market; those who do become employed often leave their positions to have greater autonomy.

The digital workforce has also placed demands on human resources. While many companies want their employees to work in-person, the convenience of working at home and the drudgery of commuting to work have created an environment where employees seek greater flexibility. Changes are coming. The employee talent challenge is likely to create a more global workforce where companies look for less expensive online talent from a pool of eager workers in other countries.

CHAPTER 13

NEXT STEPS: PREPARATION AND REAL WORLD SKILLS

"What is the recipe for successful achievement? Choose a career you love. Give it the best there is in you. Seize your opportunities. And be a member of the team."

– Benjamin Franklin Fairless

BOLD NETWORKING

Networking takes social skills and a bit of moxie. From elevator speeches and restaurant encounters to tradeshows and industry meetings, your job is to find a way to get in front of people. How can you be recognized? Meet people, hand out your resume, give them your business card, ask for their business card, follow up, ask if you can call or meet them, even when the instance may be uncomfortable to some. Stay in touch with people you meet, even if it is just happenstance or serendipity. Keep a log with each person's phone, e-mail, identifying information, and both date and location where you met. You never know when you will need it.

STAY IN TOUCH

Do not annoy busy people, but you can keep in touch every couple of months. Communicating more frequently is overwhelming. However, life is long, and, in this industry, contacts are important in all phases of your career. Also, do not be surprised if the go-getters who are also interviewing or the other interns you meet do not turn out to be very successful. People tend to only want to stay in touch with the "important" people. Note: your contemporaries or peers are important people…although not yet. Remember that as you form your lists of people, you will stay in touch with them throughout your career.

Even if you decide to work elsewhere after you interview at a few places, do not lose touch with people and do not burn bridges along the way. This industry is not that big, and you will continually see movers and shakers on all levels of the fashion world. You never know. They may contact you to collaborate one day or meet for coffee at an event. Networking is a two-way street, and the best networkers know this.

COLLEGE AND CAREER CENTERS

Almost every college has a career center. There may be a specific career liaison in the fashion, fashion design, merchandising, business, or art department. Contact them for help in your search process. Not only can they assist with resume and cover letter services, but they may have contacts in the industry. Past graduates who are in the fashion industry make great connections. They have been through the ropes, they know a few people, and they might be able to get you an interview or into a fashion industry event. Any contact may be able to get your foot into the door.

LINKEDIN

LinkedIn is especially helpful for career searches. You can find numerous influential contacts on LinkedIn. After each interview, connect with them on LinkedIn. Keep a contact list of individuals you know in the fashion industry. Do not constantly try to connect with people you do not really know. However, if you have made the connection, occasionally keep in touch.

While some LinkedIn message boxes may be full and you may not get a reply, you can try. Occasionally, you hit on a lucky break. Though I do not have time to communicate with everyone, I have connected with some of my most inspiring authors, advisors, and intellectual leaders through LinkedIn.

FINALLY

Most people are willing to help you. Five percent will not. Thus, you have a 19 out of 20 chance of interacting with decent people who have the time and will give you advice. Don't lose faith in humanity just because you ran into a few people who are too busy to stop for you or are too self-absorbed that they cannot answer your question.

- Work ethic is everything.
- Excellence is expected.
- Learn what you do not know on your own time.
- Come to work prepared.
- Take constructive criticism well.
- Keep your cool under pressure.
- Avoid being timid.
- Stay on task.
- Come early.
- Stay late.
- Take your work seriously.
- Do more than expected.
- Read your e-mail/texts after hours in case something is important.
- Ask questions. No question is too stupid.
- Maintain a clean workspace.
- Dress and act professionally.
- Don't gossip or complain.
- Avoid frustrating your phenomenally busy supervisor.
- Be straightforward, and don't beat around the bush.

You've Got This!

4
Regions

56
Programs

COLLEGE PROFILES AND REQUIREMENTS

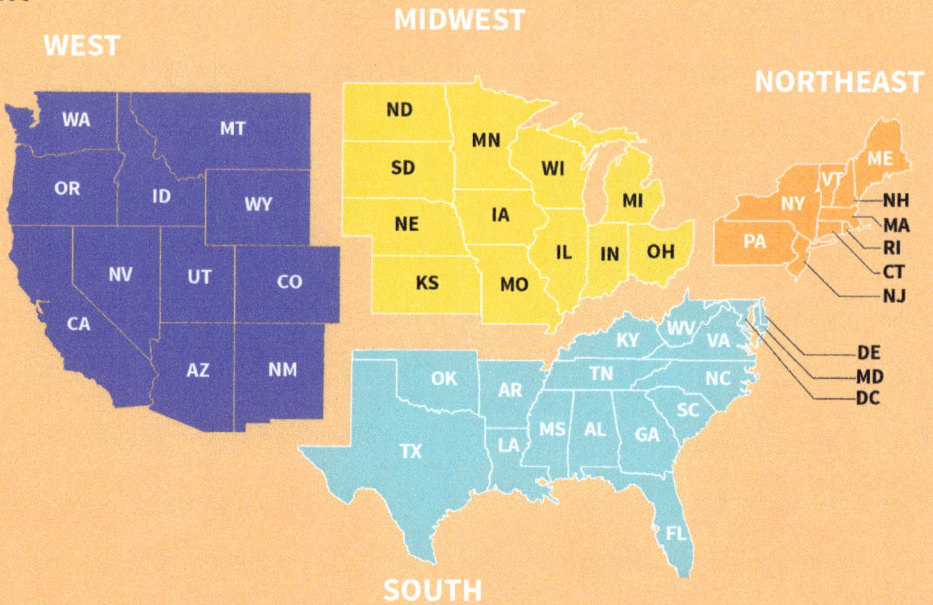

WEST

MIDWEST

NORTHEAST

SOUTH

PROGRAMS BY REGION
U.S. CENSUS BUREAU CLASSIFICATIONS

REGION 1 – NORTHEAST

Connecticut, Maine, Massachusetts, New Hampshire, New Jersey, New York, Pennsylvania, Rhode Island, and Vermont

REGION 2 – MIDWEST

Illinois, Indiana, Iowa, Kansas, Michigan, Minnesota, Missouri, Nebraska, North Dakota, Ohio, South Dakota, and Wisconsin

REGION 3 – SOUTH

Alabama, Arkansas, Delaware, District of Columbia, Florida, Georgia, Kentucky, Louisiana, Maryland, Mississippi, North Carolina, Oklahoma, South Carolina, Tennessee, Texas, Virginia, and West Virginia

REGION 4 – WEST

Alaska, Arizona, California, Colorado, Hawaii, Idaho, Montana, Nevada, New Mexico, Oregon, Utah, Washington, and Wyoming

LIST OF FASHION DESIGN PROGRAMS

The programs listed in the following pages include top fashion design programs. In addition, this book also lists the top costume design, fashion merchandising, and fashion photography programs. Many students interested in fashion are often also interested in the artistic side of clothing design, presentation, and marketing. There are many facets of the fashion/clothing design world. One of these other areas might be a good option for you.

Fashion design is not for everyone. Although immensely rewarding, there are challenges. You might choose an alternative path somewhere down the road.

Thus, this book aims to provide you with a more comprehensive set of lists so that you can explore your options. Keep the book handy. Even after you begin college, you may find the additional programs in the back are helpful for connections or summer programs.

Creating lists is often tedious and cumbersome. These lists were gathered to help you with this task.

These descriptions of the college programs, tuition, requirements, and deadlines are accurate as of February 2022. The requirements may have changed somewhat by the time you purchase this book, but this information is a great place to start!

Note: To simplify the text and fit information into the charts and descriptions, abbreviations were used as well as shortened sentences and acronyms.

CONNECTICUT

MAINE

MASSACHUSETTS

NEW HAMPSHIRE

NEW JERSEY

NEW YORK

PENNSYLVANIA

RHODE ISLAND

VERMONT

CHAPTER 14

REGION ONE

NORTHEAST

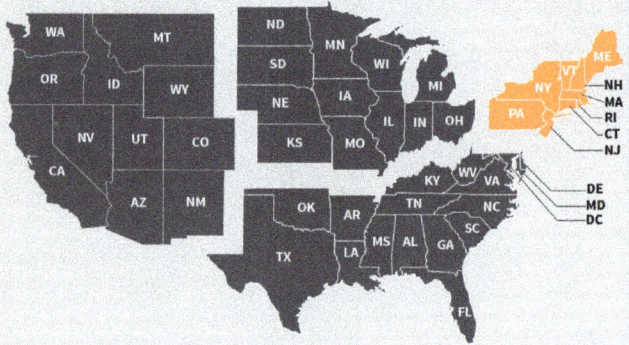

12 Programs | 9 States

1. MA - Massachusetts College of Art & Design (MassArt)
2. NY - Cornell University
3. NY - Fashion Inst. of Tech (FIT)
4. NY - Marist College
5. NY - Parsons - The New School
6. NY - Pratt Institute
7. NY - Syracuse University
8. PA - Drexel University
9. PA - Moore College of Art & Design
10. PA - Thomas Jefferson University
11. RI - Rhode Island School of Design (RISD)
12. RI - University of Rhode Island

School	Avg. GPA, SAT Evidence-Based Reading Writing (ERW), SAT Math (M), and ACT Compo / Early Decision (ED): Yes/No	Admission Statistics	Program(s)	Portfolio and/ or Interview Required (Req.)
Massachusetts College of Art & Design(MassArt) 621 Huntington Ave, Boston, MA 02115	GPA: N/A SAT (ERW): N/A SAT (M): N/A ACT (C): N/A *MassArt is test optional. ED: No	Admit Rate: 70% Undergrad Enrollment: 1,770 Total Enrollment: 1,894 Program Completion (2020): 28	BFA Fashion Design BFA Fibers	Portfolio: Req. Interview: Not req.
Cornell University 430 College Ave., Ithaca, NY 14850	GPA: N/A SAT (ERW): 680-750 SAT (M): 720-790 ACT (C): 32-35 ED: No	Admit Rate: 11% Undergrad Enrollment: 14,743 Total Enrollment: 23,620 Program Completion (2020): N/A	BS in Fashion Design & Management, option: Fashion Design BS in Fiber Science	Portfolio: Req. for Fashion Design, not req. for Fiber Science Interview: Not req.
Fashion Institute of Technology (FIT) 227 West 27th Street, New York City, NY 10001	GPA: N/A SAT (ERW): N/A SAT (M): N/A ACT (C): N/A *FIT is test optional. ED: No	Admit Rate: 59% Undergrad Enrollment: 7,959 Total Enrollment: 8,191 Program Completion (2020): 239	BFA in Fabric Styling BFA in Fashion Design BFA in Footwear and Accessories AAS in Menswear AAS in Textile Surface Design	Portfolio: Req. Interview: Not req.

FASHION DESIGN PROGRAMS

School	Avg. GPA, SAT Evidence-Based Reading Writing (ERW), SAT Math (M), and ACT Compo Early Decision (ED): Yes/No	Admission Statistics	Program(s)	Portfolio and/or Interview Required (Req.)
Marist College 3399 North Road, Poughkeepsie, NY 12601	GPA: 3.4 SAT (ERW): 580-660 SAT (M): 560-660 ACT (C): 26-31 *Marist College is test optional. ED: No	Admit Rate: 55% Undergrad Enrollment: 5,682 Total Enrollment: 6,600 Program Completion (2020): 20	BFA in Fashion Design	Portfolio: Req. Interview: Not req.
Parsons - The New School 66 Fifth Avenue, New York, NY 10011	GPA: N/A SAT (ERW): 580-680 SAT (M): 560-680 ACT (C): 26-30 ED: No	Admit Rate: 69% Undergrad Enrollment: 6,399 Total Enrollment: 9,047 Program Completion (2020): 258	BFA in Fashion Design, pathways: Collection Fashion Product Materiality Systems and Society	Portfolio: Req. Interview: Not req.
Pratt Institute 200 Willoughby Avenue, Brooklyn, NY 11205	GPA: 3.82 SAT (ERW): 570-660 SAT (M): 550-680 ACT (C): 25-30 ED: No	Admit Rate: 66% Undergrad Enrollment: 3,122 Total Enrollment: 4,353 Program Completion (2020): 54	BFA in Fashion Design	Portfolio: Req. Interview: Not req.

NORTHEAST

School	Avg. GPA, SAT Evidence-Based Reading Writing (ERW), SAT Math (M), and ACT Compo Early Decision (ED): Yes/No	Admission Statistics	Program(s)	Portfolio and/or Interview Required (Req.)
Syracuse University 900 South Crouse Ave Syracuse, NY 13244	GPA: 3.67 SAT (ERW): 580-670 SAT (M): 600-710 ACT (C): 26-30 ED: Yes	Admit Rate: 69% Undergrad Enrollment: 14,479 Total Enrollment: 21,322 Program Completion (2020): 12	BFA in Fashion Design	Portfolio: Req. Interview: Not req.
Drexel University 3250 Chestnut Street, MacAlister Hall, Suite 4020, Philadelphia, PA 19104	GPA: N/A SAT (ERW): 590-680 SAT (M): 590-700 ACT (C): 25-31 ED: No	Admit Rate: 77% Undergrad Enrollment: 14,616 Total Enrollment: 23,589 Program Completion (2020): 23	BS in Fashion Design	Portfolio: Req. Interview: Not req.
Moore College of Art & Design 1916 Race St, Philadelphia, PA 19103	GPA: N/A SAT (ERW): N/A SAT (M): N/A ACT (C): N/A *Moore College of Art & Design is test optional. ED: No	Admit Rate: 50% Undergrad Enrollment: 365 Total Enrollment: 389 Program Completion (2020): 12	BFA in Fashion Design BFA in Fashion Design + MA in Socially Engaged Art (4+1)	Portfolio: Req. Interview: Not req.

School	Avg. GPA, SAT Evidence-Based Reading Writing (ERW), SAT Math (M), and ACT Compo Early Decision (ED): Yes/No	Admission Statistics	Program(s)	Portfolio and/or Interview Required (Req.)
Thomas Jefferson University 4201 Henry Avenue, Philadelphia, PA 19144	GPA: N/A SAT (ERW): 550-630 SAT (M): 540-640 ACT (C): 20-27 ED: No	Admit Rate: 70% Undergrad Enrollment: 3,783 Total Enrollment: 8,286 Program Completion (2020): 31	BS in Fashion Design	Portfolio: Optional Interview: Not req.
Rhode Island School of Design (RISD) 2 College St, Providence, RI 02903	GPA: N/A SAT (ERW): 610-700 SAT (M): 640-770 ACT (C): 27-32 ED: Yes	Admit Rate: 27% Undergrad Enrollment: 1,736 Total Enrollment: 2,227 Program Completion (2020): 49	BFA in Apparel Design	Portfolio: Req. Interview: Not req.
University of Rhode Island 35 Campus Avenue, Kingston, Rhode Island 02881	GPA: 3.56 SAT (ERW): 550-630 SAT (M): 540-630 ACT (C): 23-28 ED: No	Admit Rate: 76% Undergrad Enrollment: 14,904 Total Enrollment: 17,649 Program Completion (2020): 60	BS in Textiles, Fashion Merchandising, and Design, concentrations: Apparel Design Textile Science Accelerated 4+1 BS/MS in Textiles, Fashion Merchandising, and Design	Portfolio: Not req. Interview: Not req.

NORTHEAST

CONNECTICUT

MAINE

MASSACHUSETTS

NEW HAMPSHIRE

NEW JERSEY

NEW YORK

PENNSYLVANIA

RHODE ISLAND

VERMONT

MASSACHUSETTS COLLEGE OF ART & DESIGN (MassArt)

Address: 621 Huntington Ave, Boston, MA 02115
Website: https://massart.edu/academics/programs/fashion-design
Contact: https://massart.edu/contactus
Request for Information: https://massart.edu/request-information
Phone: (617) 879-7000
Email: admissions@massart.edu

COST OF ATTENDANCE:

In-State Tuition & Fees: $14,200 | **Additional Expenses:** $19,200
Total: $33,400

New England Resident: $31,800| **Additional Expenses:** $19,200
Total: $51,000

Out-of-State Tuition & Fees: $39,800 | **Additional Expenses:** $19,200
Total: $59,000

Financial Aid: https://massart.edu/financial-aid

ADDITIONAL INFORMATION:

Available Degree(s)

- BFA Fashion Design
- BFA Fibers

Freshman Portfolio Requirement

Submit via the Common Application

- Submit 15-20 examples of best and most recent work
- You may concentrate on a single medium or show a variety of media
- Do not include artwork that copies another artist's work
- Do not submit theater performances, musical recordings, screenplays, or creative writing samples.

For more information, visit: https://massart.edu/portfolio-tips

Scholarships Offered

All eligible applicants are automatically considered for merit scholarships. To be considered, students need to demonstrate high academic achievement and showcase a strong portfolio. Out-of-state applicants may be eligible for the MassArt Merit Scholarship, the MassArt Transfer Merit Scholarship, or the Trustees Scholarship (covers all tuition and fees, renewable for four years). In-state applicants may be considered for the MassArt Merit Scholarship, the MassArt Transfer Merit Scholarship, and the Senator Paul E. Tsongas Scholarship (covers all tuition and fees for four years). For more information, visit: https://massart.edu/scholarships

Special Opportunities

The Fashion Department collaborates with numerous companies and organizations. Projects in the past have been with Primark, Anne Fontaine, Italian Trade Commission, Levi Strauss, and more.

Notable Alumni

- Robin Chalfin: Owner, *Toolkit*

CORNELL UNIVERSITY

Address: 430 College Ave., Ithaca, NY 14850
Website: https://www.human.cornell.edu/hcd/academics/
undergraduate-study/fashion-design-and-management
Contact: https://www.human.cornell.edu/contact
Request for Information: https://admissions.cornell.edu/
requesting-information
Phone: (607) 254-2700
Email: admissions@cornell.edu

COST OF ATTENDANCE:

In-State Tuition & Fees: $40,382 | **Additional Expenses:** $20,001
Total: $60,383

Out-of-State Tuition & Fees: $60,286 | **Additional Expenses:** $20,001
Total: $80,287

***Note:** The College of Human Ecology is a State Contract College,
therefore there is an in-state tuition rate.

Financial Aid: https://finaid.cornell.edu/

ADDITIONAL INFORMATION:

Available Degree(s)

- BS in Fashion Design & Management, option: Fashion Design
- BS in Fiber Science

Freshman Portfolio Requirement
There is no portfolio requirement for the BS in Fiber Science.

BS in Fashion Design & Management, option: Fashion Design
- Submit a portfolio and a fashion design index via SlideRoom
- Fashion Design Index:
  - o 4 prompts, around 150 words each
- Portfolio:
  - o Maximum 15 examples of design work, each labeled.
  - o Two-thirds of portfolio should be "primary work".
  - o Primary work (e.g., fashion illustrations, clothing you've designed, textile design projects)
  - o Secondary work (ceramics, crafts, glasswork, paintings)

For more information, visit: https://www.human.cornell.
edu/admissions/undergraduate/fashiondesignportfolio

Scholarships Offered
Cornell does not offer any merit aid or athletic scholarships. All aid
is need-based. According to Cornell, "there is no standard 'income
bracket' or cut-off for grant aid recipients; eligibility is determined
on a case-by-case basis." Students are also automatically
considered for endowed scholarships when they apply for financial
aid. For more information, visit: https://finaid.cornell.edu/types-
aid/grants-and-scholarships

Special Opportunities
Students may be enrolled in the Fashion Science and Apparel
Design (FSAD) Honors Program. For more information, visit: https://
www.human.cornell.edu/fsad/academics/undergraduate/honors

The Department of Human Centered Design offers a minor in
Healthy Futures.

Notable Alumni
- Gizelle Begler: International Fashion
  Designer

CONNECTICUT

MAINE

MASSACHUSETTS

NEW HAMPSHIRE

NEW JERSEY

NEW YORK

PENNSYLVANIA

RHODE ISLAND

VERMONT

NORTHEAST

FASHION INSTITUTE OF TECHNOLOGY (FIT)

Address: 227 West 27th Street, New York City, NY 10001
Website: http://www.fitnyc.edu/academics/academic-divisions/art-and-design/fashion-design/degree-details/index.php
Contact: http://www.fitnyc.edu/about/contact/index.php
Request for Information: http://www.fitnyc.edu/admissions/request-information.php
Phone: (212) 217-3760
Email: fitinfo@fitnyc.edu

COST OF ATTENDANCE:

In-State Tuition & Fees: $7,920 | **Additional Expenses:** $18,556
Total: $26,476

Out-of-State Tuition & Fees: $22,242 | **Additional Expenses:** $18,556
Total: $40,798

Financial Aid: https://www.fitnyc.edu/admissions/costs/financial-aid/index.php

ADDITIONAL INFORMATION:

Available Degree(s)
- BFA in Fabric Styling
- BFA in Fashion Design
- BFA in Footwear and Accessories
- AAS in Menswear
- AAS in Textile Surface Design

Freshman Portfolio Requirement
High school students must first apply to the AAS program. Following are the materials required for the AAS Fashion Design portfolio. They must be submitted via SlideRoom.
- 250-word essay
- Project 1: Sportswear Coordinates (3-6 images): Create a mood/inspiration page for sportswear and include a short, written explanation of how the design is inspired by the mood page. List the destination and season when the designs should be worn.
- Project 2: Fashion Design Artwork (4-8 images): Original fashion design artwork on figures you have drawn yourself. Include scanned or digital photos of actual 2x2 fabric swatches and identify the fabric type.
- Project 3: Sewing Project (4-9 photographs): 2-3 garments you have sewn (include front and back views). Photograph clothing on person or dress mannequin.

Students submit BFA portfolios later. For more information, visit: http://www.fitnyc.edu/admissions/apply/portfolio/fashion-design-aas.php

Scholarships Offered
FIT scholarships are donor scholarships typically gifted to students with high financial need. The average award is $1,100. For more information, visit: https://www.fitnyc.edu/admissions/costs/financial-aid/scholarships/index.php

Special Opportunities
Fashion Design AAS students may study in Florence during their 1st or 2nd year. Fashion Design BFA students may study in Milan for their entire 3rd or 4th year.

Notable Alumni
- Calvin Klein: Founder, Calvin Klein
- Michael Kors: Founder, Michael Kors
- John Varvatos: Founder, John Varvatos

MARIST COLLEGE

Address: 3399 North Road, Poughkeepsie, NY 12601
Website: https://www.marist.edu/communication-arts/fashion
Contact: https://www.marist.edu/admission/undergraduate/counselors
Request for Information: https://www.marist.edu/request-information
Phone: (845) 575-3000
Email: admission@marist.edu

COST OF ATTENDANCE:

Tuition & Fees: $44,360 | **Additional Expenses:** $20,075
Total: $64,435

Financial Aid: https://www.marist.edu/admission/student-financial-services

ADDITIONAL INFORMATION:

Available Degree(s)
- BFA in Fashion Design

Freshman Portfolio Requirement
- Submit via SlideRoom
- Include an inspiration/mood board
- 200-word essay
- Design mix and match separates that work and can be work together in a collection
  o Option 1: Fashion Emphasis:
- Draw original garment designs in color (medium of your choice)
- Design collection of different but related mix and match separates (over 5 fashion figures)
- Fabrics and flat sketches should be included
- 4-Free Zone: submit 2 non-fashion examples of most recent work showcasing your thinking/making
  o Option 2: Art Emphasis:
- Draw original garment designs in color (medium of your choice)
- Design collection of different but related mix and match separates (over 2 fashion figures)
- Fabrics and flat sketches should be included
- 4-Free Zone: submit 3-5 non-fashion examples of most recent work showcasing your thinking/making
- Figures must not be traced
- All must be original works by the applicants by hand or via use of a computer drawing program

https://www.marist.edu/admission/undergraduate/apply/supplemental-materials

Scholarships Offered
Merit-based scholarships at Marist College range from $10,000-$25,000 per year. There is no additional application required. These awards are renewable as long as students maintain a cumulative GPA of 2.85. For more information, visit: https://www.marist.edu/admission/financial-aid/marist-scholarships

Special Opportunities
The Silver Needle Runway showcases student designers' works. Approximately 2000 people attend. A presentation of awards and scholarships follows the runway show. Awards have been provided by Kate Spade, MPorium, Cutty Sark, and Young Menswear Association, among others. For more information, visit: https://www.marist.edu/communication-arts/fashion/silver-needle-runway

CONNECTICUT

MAINE

MASSACHUSETTS

NEW HAMPSHIRE

NEW JERSEY

NEW YORK

PENNSYLVANIA

RHODE ISLAND

VERMONT

NORTHEAST

CONNECTICUT

MAINE

MASSACHUSETTS

NEW HAMPSHIRE

NEW JERSEY

NEW YORK

PENNSYLVANIA

RHODE ISLAND

VERMONT

PARSONS - THE NEW SCHOOL

Address: 66 Fifth Avenue, New York, NY 10011
Website: https://www.newschool.edu/parsons/bfa-fashion-design/
Contact: https://www.newschool.edu/parsons/contact/
Request for Information: https://www.newschool.edu/parsons/contact-admissions/
Phone: (212) 229-8900
Email: thinkparsons@newschool.edu

COST OF ATTENDANCE:

Tuition & Fees: $51,722 | **Additional Expenses:** N/A
Total: $51,722

Financial Aid: https://www.newschool.edu/financial-aid/

ADDITIONAL INFORMATION:

Available Degree(s)

- BFA in Fashion Design, pathways:
  - Collection
  - Fashion Product
  - Materiality
  - Systems and Society

Freshman Portfolio Requirement

- Applicants must submit the Parsons Challenge and a portfolio via SlideRoom
- Parsons Challenge:
  - Create new visual work inspired by theme within a piece submitted in the portfolio
  - Support process by writing 500-word essay describing your thought process
  - You may submit up to 2 additional visual pieces to demonstrate process
- Portfolio:
  - 8-12 images

For more information, visit: https://www.newschool.edu/parsons/bfa-fashion-design/?show=program-admission-requirements

Scholarships Offered

The New School offers merit-based and need-based aid to students. Students are automatically considered for merit-based scholarships. These are based on the strength of the application and portfolio. Need-based aid is available to students who are eligible and submit the FAFSA. For more information, visit: https://www.newschool.edu/financial-aid/new-school-scholarships/

Notable Alumni

- Anna Sui: "Top 5 Fashion Icons of the Decade"
- Donna Karan: Fashion Designer and Creator of Donna Karen New York (Dkny)
- Maisie Schloss: American Fashion Designer
- Isaac Mizrahi: Fashion Designer and Chief Designer of the Isaac Mizrahi brand; Judge, *Project Runway: All Stars.*
- Marc Jacobs: Fashion Designer who founded his fashion label, Marc Jacobs

PRATT INSTITUTE

Address: 200 Willoughby Avenue, Brooklyn, NY 11205
Website: https://www.pratt.edu/academics/school-of-design/
undergraduate-school-of-design/fashion/fashion-bfa/
Contact: https://www.pratt.edu/academics/school-of-design/
undergraduate-school-of-design/fashion/fashion-department-
contact/
Request for Information: https://www.applyweb.com/public/
inquiry?s=prattinq
Phone: (718) 636-3600
Email: admissions@pratt.edu

COST OF ATTENDANCE:

Tuition & Fees: $53,566 | **Additional Expenses:** $19,824
Total: $73,390

Financial Aid: https://www.pratt.edu/admissions/financing-your-
education/financing-undergraduate/

ADDITIONAL INFORMATION:

Available Degree(s)

- BFA in Fashion Design

Freshman Portfolio Requirement

- Submit via SlideRoom
- 12-20 pieces of best and most recent work
- Include 3-5 drawings from observation
- Do not include work that copies photos, uses the grid system, or copies others' works (e.g., cartoons)

For more information, visit: https://www.pratt.edu/admissions/
applying/applying-undergraduate/ug-application-requirements/
freshman-and-transfer-portfolio-requirements/

Scholarships Offered

Pratt offers merit-based and endowed scholarships in addition
to need-based grants. Furthermore, there are merit-based
scholarships available to international students as well. The
Presidential Merit-Based Scholarships are available to all Pratt
students in varied award amounts. For more information, visit:
https://www.pratt.edu/admissions/financing-your-education/
financing-undergraduate/financial-aid-options/ug-financial-
scholarships/

Special Opportunities

All Pratt students must complete 3 internship credits during their
senior year. Students explore the New York fashion design industry
and learn how to present their portfolio.

Notable Alumni

- Betsey Johnson: Fashion Designer known for her whimsical designs.
- Vera Maxwell: Sportswear and Fashion Designer.
- Norman Norell: Fashion Designer known for his elegant gowns and suits.

CONNECTICUT

MAINE

MASSACHUSETTS

NEW HAMPSHIRE

NEW JERSEY

NEW YORK

PENNSYLVANIA

RHODE ISLAND

VERMONT

NORTHEAST

CONNECTICUT

MAINE

MASSACHUSETTS

NEW HAMPSHIRE

NEW JERSEY

NEW YORK

PENNSYLVANIA

RHODE ISLAND

VERMONT

SYRACUSE UNIVERSITY

Address: 200 Crouse College, Syracuse, NY 13244
Website: https://vpa.syr.edu/academics/design/programs/fashion-design-bfa/
Contact: https://vpa.syr.edu/academics/drama/contact/
Request for Information: https://vpa.syr.edu/admissions/request-information/
Phone: (315) 443-2769
Email: admissu@syr.edu

COST OF ATTENDANCE:

Tuition & Fees: $55,920 | **Additional Expenses:** $24,119
Total: $80,039

Financial Aid: https://www.syracuse.edu/admissions/cost-and-aid/

ADDITIONAL INFORMATION:

Available Degree(s)

- BFA in Fashion Design

Freshman Portfolio Requirement

- Submit via SlideRoom - either a traditional portfolio or an alternative portfolio
- Traditional Portfolio
- 12-20 images of most recent work
- Include fashion-related works
- 1 short answer question (200 words max)
- 1 writing sample (500 words)
- Alternative Portfolio
- Written exercise (500 words)
- 2D exercise
- 3D exercise

For more information, visit: https://vpa.syr.edu/admissions/undergraduate/art-design-transmedia/

Scholarships Offered

Syracuse University offers various merit-based and need-based scholarships and grants including the 1870 Scholarship (full tuition). Artistic Scholarships are awarded to students based on talent and require a maintained cumulative GPA of 2.75+. The Distinguished Art Portfolio Award offers $10,000 awards annually. There is also the Tepper Semester Grant. For more information, visit: https://financialaid.syr.edu/scholarships/

Special Opportunities

Students learn technical skills by utilizing Optitex CAD and Adobe Suite. Furthermore, students may participate in a professional semester in London, England with the London College of Fashion.

Notable Alumni

- Betsey Johnson: Fashion Designer, Medal of Honor for Lifetime Achievement in Fashion

DREXEL UNIVERSITY

Address: 3141 Chestnut Street, Philadelphia, PA 19104
Website: https://drexel.edu/westphal/academics/undergraduate/
FASH/
Contact: https://drexel.edu/westphal/about/contact/
Request for Information: https://drexel.edu/westphal/admissions/
request-information/
Phone: (215) 895-2000
Email: westphal.admissions@drexel.edu

COST OF ATTENDANCE:

Tuition & Fees: $57,171 | **Additional Expenses:** $19,388
Total: $76,559

Financial Aid: https://drexel.edu/drexelcentral/finaid/overview/

ADDITIONAL INFORMATION:

Available Degree(s)

- BS in Fashion Design

Freshman Portfolio Requirement

- Submit via SlideRoom
- 8-12 pieces of strongest and most recent work in variety of media
- Drawings from observation encouraged
- Students may attend a portfolio review day

For more information, visit: https://drexel.edu/undergrad/apply/
freshmen-instructions/

Scholarships Offered

Westphal Portfolio Scholarship available to incoming first-year students based on outstanding portfolio work. Amount awarded is not listed. In addition, merit-based awards and other scholarships are available. For more information, visit: https://drexel.edu/
drexelcentral/finaid/grants/undergraduate-scholarships/

Special Opportunities

Fashion Design majors utilize the URBN Center. This facility houses spacious studios with 24/7 access. Students have access to 3D printers, laser cutters, Shima Seiki knitting machines, and computer simulation and cutting-edge software. The URBN Center also houses the Richard & Penny Fox Historic Costume Collection. This collection contains over 17,000 fashion items.

The College of Media Arts & Design offers a BS in Design & Merchandising. There is also an accelerated dual degree program, where students earn their BS in Design & Merchandising and a MBA in five years. For more information, visit: http://catalog.drexel.
edu/undergraduate/collegeofmediaartsanddesign/design-and-
merchandising_bsmba/index.html

CONNECTICUT

MAINE

MASSACHUSETTS

NEW HAMPSHIRE

NEW JERSEY

NEW YORK

PENNSYLVANIA

RHODE ISLAND

VERMONT

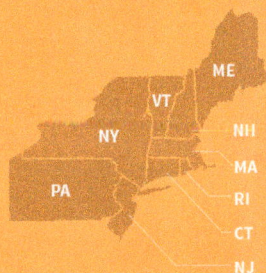

NORTHEAST

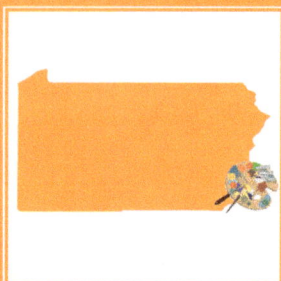

CONNECTICUT

MAINE

MASSACHUSETTS

NEW HAMPSHIRE

NEW JERSEY

NEW YORK

PENNSYLVANIA

RHODE ISLAND

VERMONT

MOORE COLLEGE OF ART & DESIGN

Address: 1916 Race Street, Philadelphia, PA 19103
Website: https://moore.edu/academics/undergraduate-studies/
programs/fashion-design/
Contact: https://moore.edu/about-moore/contact-us
Request for Information: https://admissions.moore.edu/register/
degreeinquiry
Phone: (215) 965-4000
Email: info@moore.edu

COST OF ATTENDANCE:

Tuition & Fees: $44,620 | **Additional Expenses:** $16,188
Total: $60,808

Financial Aid: https://moore.edu/admissions-aid/tuition-financial-
aid/

ADDITIONAL INFORMATION:

Available Degree(s)

- BFA in Fashion Design
- BFA in Fashion Design + MA in Socially Engaged Art (4+1)

Freshman Portfolio Requirement

- Submit via SlideRoom
- 8-12 pieces of best work created in past 1-2 years
- Variety of media preferred
- Highly recommended that some examples of direct
  observational drawings are included

For more information, visit: https://moore.edu/admissions-aid/
undergraduate-students/how-to-apply/portfolio-requirements/

Scholarships Offered

Scholarships include, but are not limited to, the Trustees
Scholarship (up to $20,000 per year), the Presidential Scholarship
(up to $17,000 per year), the Dean's Scholarship (up to $14,000 per
year), and the Admissions Scholarship (up to $8,000 per year). In
addition, the International Scholarship is a $20,000 award available
to international students on the basis of academic achievement
and the TOEFL score. Moore College of Art & Design also offers
competitive scholarships for new students, ranging from $1,000 to
$22,000. For more information, visit: https://moore.edu/admissions/
bfa-admissions/tuition-and-financial-aid/scholarships

Special Opportunities

Moore offers a unique, 4+1 BFA + MA program. Students may
choose to earn their BFA and MA in Art Education with an Emphasis
in Inclusive Practices, or choose a BFA in any major and an MA in
Socially Engaged Art. For more information on the 4+1 Program,
visit: https://moore.edu/academics/undergraduate-studies/4-1-
program/

THOMAS JEFFERSON UNIVERSITY

Address: 4201 Henry Avenue, Philadelphia, PA 19144
Website: https://www.jefferson.edu/academics/colleges-schools-institutes/kanbar-college-of-design-engineering-commerce/school-of-design-engineering.html
Contact: https://www.jefferson.edu/university/contact.html
Request for Information: http://www.eastfalls.jefferson.edu/undergrad/Contact/requestinfo.html
Phone: (215) 951-2800
Email: Admissions@PhilaU.edu

COST OF ATTENDANCE:

Tuition & Fees: $42,966 | **Additional Expenses:** $14,949
Total: $57,925

Financial Aid: https://www.jefferson.edu/tuition-and-financial-aid.html

ADDITIONAL INFORMATION:

Available Degree(s)

- BS in Fashion Design

Freshman Portfolio Requirement

- Portfolios are optional
- Submission location depends on if application is completed through Common App vs. MyJefferson App
- 3-5 works
- Drawings from observation encouraged

For more information, visit: https://www.jefferson.edu/admissions/undergraduate/first-year/apply/portfolio-submission.html

Scholarships Offered

Various merit-based, athletic, and endowed scholarships available. Merit awards range from $4,000 to $19,000 for incoming freshmen. For more information, visit: https://www.eastfalls.jefferson.edu/financialaid/Undergraduate/scholarships/index.html

Special Opportunities

Students may attend the semester study abroad program in Rome at the Center for Architecture and Fashion at UARC. Thomas Jefferson University also has partnerships with programs in Milan, Tokyo, and Paris. For more information, visit: https://www.jefferson.edu/academics/colleges-schools-institutes/kanbar-college-of-design-engineering-commerce/school-of-design-engineering/academic-programs/fashion-design/study-abroad.html

CONNECTICUT

MAINE

MASSACHUSETTS

NEW HAMPSHIRE

NEW JERSEY

NEW YORK

PENNSYLVANIA

RHODE ISLAND

VERMONT

NORTHEAST

CONNECTICUT

MAINE

MASSACHUSETTS

NEW HAMPSHIRE

NEW JERSEY

NEW YORK

PENNSYLVANIA

RHODE ISLAND

VERMONT

RHODE ISLAND SCHOOL OF DESIGN (RISD)

Address: 2 College St, Providence, RI 02903
Website: https://www.risd.edu/academics/apparel-design/bachelors-program
Contact: https://www.risd.edu/academics/apparel-design/contact/
Request for Information: N/A
Phone: (401) 454-6300
Email: admissions@risd.edu

COST OF ATTENDANCE:

Tuition & Fees: $55,220 | **Additional Expenses:** $22,060
Total: $77,280

Financial Aid: https://www.risd.edu/student-financial-services/undergraduate-aid/

ADDITIONAL INFORMATION:

Available Degree(s)

- BFA in Apparel Design

Freshman Portfolio Requirement

- Submit via SlideRoom
- 12-20 examples of most recent work
- Strongly recommend including examples of drawing from direct observation
- Up to three works may be research/preparatory work
- "The Assignment": Choose a paired concept and make a work based on the prompt

For more information, visit: https://www.risd.edu/admissions/first-year/apply/

Scholarships Offered

RISD scholarships are need-based. Students must submit a FAFSA application each year to be considered. RISD is also partnered with Scholarship Universe, a website that matches students with outside scholarships and keeps students on track with deadlines. For more information on available scholarships, visit: https://www.risd.edu/student-financial-services/undergraduate-aid/

Special Opportunities

Brown University and the Rhode Island School of Design (RISD) offer a joint, dual degree program for students who wish to earn their BA/BS-BFA. This five-year program requires separate applications to RISD and Brown. For more information, visit: https://www.brown.edu/academics/brown-risd-dual-degree/prospective-students

RISD houses numerous facilities and resources that students may gain access to. Equipment includes 40 industrial sewing machines, 3 industrial zig-zag sewing machines, 8 sergers, 2 coverstitch machines, one walking foot (leather) machine, one Makerbot 3D printer, and 18 Brother knitting machines, among other types of equipment. For more information, visit: https://www.risd.edu/academics/apparel-design/workspaces-tools/

Notable Alumni

- Nicole Miller: CEO, Nicole Miller

UNIVERSITY OF RHODE ISLAND

Address: 35 Campus Avenue, Kingston, RI 02881
Website: https://web.uri.edu/business/about/tmd/
Contact: https://www.uri.edu/about/contact/
Request for Information: https://admissions.uri.edu/register/request-information
Phone: (401) 874-7000
Email: admission@uri.edu

COST OF ATTENDANCE:

In-State Tuition & Fees: $13,792 | **Additional Expenses:** $15,693
Total: $29,485

Out-of-State Tuition & Fees: $30,042 | **Additional Expenses:** $15,693
Total: $45,735

Financial Aid: https://web.uri.edu/enrollment/financial-aid/

ADDITIONAL INFORMATION:

Available Degree(s)

- BS in Textiles, Fashion Merchandising, and Design, concentrations:
  - Apparel Design
  - Textile Science
- Accelerated 4+1 BS/MS in Textiles, Fashion Merchandising, and Design

Freshman Portfolio Requirement

There is no portfolio requirement.

Scholarships Offered

All applicants who submit their applications by December 1 will be automatically considered for scholarships. Eligibility is based on merit. The Thomas M. Ryan Scholars Program awards the full cost of attendance for all four years. In addition, students receive access to the Honors Program and Colloquium, Leadership Institute, priority course registration, a yearly donor retreat, and many other perks. First-year applicants may also be eligible for the URI Presidential Scholarship, which ranges in value from $1,500- $15,000 per year or the URI University Scholarship, which ranges from $2,000-$10,000. For more information, visit: https://web.uri.edu/admission/first-year/scholarships-and-honors/

Special Opportunities

URI houses a library archive of 40,000+ commercial patterns and the Historic Textile and Costume Collection of 20,000+ items – one of the best collections in the country.

Students may be interested in the Accelerated BS to MS degree in Textiles, Fashion Merchandising, and Design. For more information on the 4+1 degree, visit: https://web.uri.edu/business/accelerated-b-s-to-m-s-in-textiles-fashion-merchandising-and-design/

CONNECTICUT

MAINE

MASSACHUSETTS

NEW HAMPSHIRE

NEW JERSEY

NEW YORK

PENNSYLVANIA

RHODE ISLAND

VERMONT

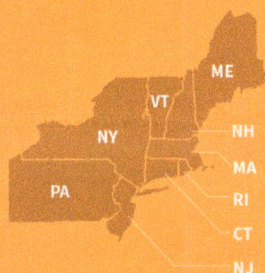

NORTHEAST

ILLINOIS

INDIANA

IOWA

KANSAS

MICHIGAN

MINNESOTA

MISSOURI

NEBRASKA

NORTH DAKOTA

OHIO

SOUTH DAKOTA

WISCONSIN

CHAPTER 15

REGION TWO

MIDWEST

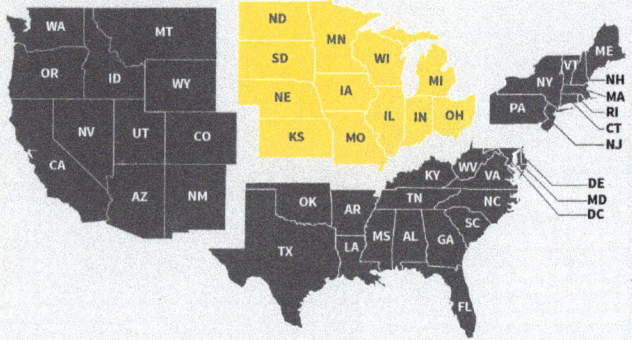

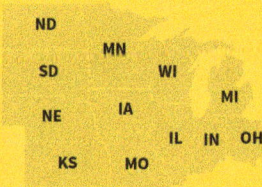

14 Programs | 12 States

1. IL - Columbia College Chicago
2. IL - Dominican University
3. IL - School of the Art Institute of Chicago (SAIC)
4. IN - Indiana University Bloomington
5. IA - Iowa State University
6. KS - Kansas State University
7. MI - Michigan State University
8. MN - University of Minnesota
9. MO - Stephens College
10. MO - Washington University in St. Louis
11. NE - University of Nebraska
12. OH - Columbus College of Art & Design
13. OH - Kent State University
14. OH - University of Cincinnati

FASHION DESIGN PROGRAMS

School	Avg. GPA, SAT Evidence-Based Reading Writing (ERW), SAT Math (M), and ACT Composite (C) Early Decision (ED): Yes/No	Admission Statistics	Program(s)	Portfolio and/ or Interview Required (Req.)
Columbia College Chicago 600 S. Michigan Avenue, Chicago, IL 60605	GPA: N/A SAT (ERW): N/A SAT (M): N/A ACT (C): N/A *Columbia College Chicago is test optional. ED: No	Admit Rate: 90% Undergrad Enrollment: 6,542 Total Enrollment: 6,769 Program Completion (2020): 66	BA in Fashion Studies, concentration: Product Development BFA in Fashion Design	Portfolio: Req. for BFA, optional for BA Interview: Req for BFA, not req. for BA
Dominican University 7900 West Division Street, River Forest, IL 60305	GPA: 3.72 SAT (ERW): 480-580 SAT (M): 480-580 ACT (C): 19-24 ED: No	Admit Rate: 76% Undergrad Enrollment: 2,166 Total Enrollment: 3,189 Program Completion (2020): 8	BA in Fashion Design	Portfolio: Not req. Interview: Not req.
School of the Art Institute of Chicago (SAIC) 36 S. Wabash Ave., Chicago, IL 60603	GPA: N/A SAT (ERW): 560-660 SAT (M): 480-600 ACT (C): 22-25 ED: No	Admit Rate: 78% Undergrad Enrollment: 2,487 Total Enrollment: 3,132 Program Completion (2020): N/A	BFA in Fashion Design BFA in Fiber and Material Studies	Portfolio: Req. Interview: Not req.

FASHION DESIGN PROGRAMS

School	Avg. GPA, SAT Evidence-Based Reading Writing (ERW), SAT Math (M), and ACT Composite (C) Early Decision (ED): Yes/No	Admission Statistics	Program(s)	Portfolio and/or Interview Required (Req.)
Indiana University at Bloomington 107 S. Indiana Avenue, Bloomington, IN 47405	GPA: 3.75 SAT (ERW): 560-670 SAT (M): 560-680 ACT (C): 24-31 *Indiana University at Bloomington is test optional. ED: No	Admit Rate: 80% Undergrad Enrollment: 32,986 Total Enrollment: 43,064 Program Completion (2020): 17	BA in Fashion Design	Portfolio: Not req. Interview: Not req.
Iowa State University 715 Bissell Rd., Ames, IA 50011	GPA: 3.71 SAT (ERW): 480-630 SAT (M): 530-680 ACT (C): 21-28 ED: No	Admit Rate: 88% Undergrad Enrollment: 26,843 Total Enrollment: 31,822 Program Completion (2020): N/A	BS in Apparel, Merchandising, and Design, option: Creative and Technical Design	Portfolio: Not req. Interview: Not req.
Kansas State University 225 Justin Hall, 1324 Lovers Lane, Manhattan, KS 66506	GPA: 3.62 SAT (ERW): N/A SAT (M): N/A ACT (C): 20-27 *Kansas State University is test optional. ED: No	Admit Rate: 94% Undergrad Enrollment: 16,257 Total Enrollment: 20,854 Program Completion (2020): 58	BS in Fashion Studies, specialization: Fashion Design	Portfolio: Not req. Interview: Not req.

MIDWEST

FASHION DESIGN PROGRAMS

School	Avg. GPA, SAT Evidence-Based Reading Writing (ERW), SAT Math (M), and ACT Composite (C) Early Decision (ED): Yes/No	Admission Statistics	Program(s)	Portfolio and/or Interview Required (Req.)
Michigan State University Michigan State University, East Lansing, MI 48824	GPA: 3.74 SAT (ERW): 550-640 SAT (M): 550-660 ACT (C): 23-29 ED: No	Admit Rate: 76% Undergrad Enrollment: 38,491 Total Enrollment: 49,695 Program Completion (2020): 28	BA in Apparel & Textile Design BFA in Apparel & Textile Design	Portfolio: Req. Interview: Not req.
University of Minnesota 107 Rapson Hall, 89 Church Street SE, Minneapolis, MN 55455	GPA: N/A SAT (ERW): 600-700 SAT (M): 640-760 ACT (C): 25-31 ED: No	Admit Rate: 70% Undergrad Enrollment: 36,061 Total Enrollment: 52,017 Program Completion (2020): 15	BS in Apparel Design	Portfolio: Not req. Interview: Not req.
Stephens College 1200 E Broadway, Columbia, MO 65215	GPA: N/A SAT (ERW): 600-700 SAT (M): 640-760 ACT (C): 25-31 ED: No	Admit Rate: 64% Undergrad Enrollment: 443 Total Enrollment: 622 Program Completion (2020): 9	BA in Apparel Studies BFA in Fashion Design and Product Development	Portfolio: Not req. Interview: Not req.

FASHION DESIGN PROGRAMS

School	Avg. GPA, SAT Evidence-Based Reading Writing (ERW), SAT Math (M), and ACT Composite (C) Early Decision (ED): Yes/No	Admission Statistics	Program(s)	Portfolio and/or Interview Required (Req.)
Washington Univ. in St. Louis 1 Brookings Dr., St. Louis, MO 63130	GPA: 4.21 SAT (ERW): 720-760 SAT (M): 760-800 ACT (C): 33-35 ED: Yes	Admit Rate: 16% Undergrad Enrollment: 7,653 Total Enrollment: 15,449 Program Completion (2020): 8	BFA in Fashion Design BA in Design, concentration: Fashion Design	Portfolio: Req. Interview: Not req.
University of Nebraska 4th and R St, Lincoln, NE 68588	GPA: 3.6 SAT (ERW): 550-650 SAT (M): 560-670 ACT (C): 22-28 ED: No	Admit Rate: 78% Undergrad Enrollment: 20,286 Total Enrollment: 25,108 Program Completion (2020): 14	BS in Textiles & Apparel Design BS in Textiles, Merchandising, & Fashion Design/Communications BS in Textile Science	Portfolio: Not req. Interview: Not req.
Columbus College of Art and Design 60 Cleveland Ave, Columbus, OH 43215	GPA: N/A SAT (ERW): N/A SAT (M): N/A ACT (C): N/A *Columbus College of Art and Design is test optional. ED: No	Admit Rate: 92% Undergrad Enrollment: 982 Total Enrollment: 1,009 Program Completion (2020): 13	BFA Fashion Design	Portfolio: Req. Interview: Not req.

MIDWEST

FASHION DESIGN PROGRAMS

School	Avg. GPA, SAT Evidence-Based Reading Writing (ERW), SAT Math (M), and ACT Composite (C) Early Decision (ED): Yes/No	Admission Statistics	Program(s)	Portfolio and/or Interview Required (Req.)
Kent State University 515 Hilltop Drive, Kent, OH 44242	GPA: 3.61 SAT (ERW): 510-610 SAT (M): 510-600 ACT (C): 20-26 ED: No	Admit Rate: 84% Undergrad Enrollment: 21,621 Total Enrollment: 26,822 Program Completion (2020): 100	BA in Fashion Design BFA in Fashion Design	Portfolio: Req. Interview: Not req.
University of Cincinnati 2600 Clifton Ave, Cincinnati, OH 45221	GPA: 3.7 SAT (ERW): 560-650 SAT (M): 560-680 ACT (C): 23-29 ED: No	Admit Rate: 76% Undergrad Enrollment: 29,933 Total Enrollment: 40,826 Program Completion (2020): 38	BSDES in Fashion Design	Portfolio: Optional Interview: Not req.

COLUMBIA COLLEGE CHICAGO

Address: 600 S. Michigan Avenue, Chicago, IL 60605
Website: https://www.colum.edu/academics/programs/fashion-studies
Contact: https://www.colum.edu/contact
Request for Information: https://apply.colum.edu/register/moreinfo
Phone: (312) 369-1000
Email: admissions@colum.edu

COST OF ATTENDANCE:

Tuition & Fees: $35,716 | **Additional Expenses:** $18,000
Total: $53,716

Financial Aid: https://www.colum.edu/columbia-central/where-to-start/index

ILLINOIS

INDIANA

IOWA

KANSAS

MICHIGAN

MINNESOTA

MISSOURI

NEBRASKA

NORTH DAKOTA

OHIO

SOUTH DAKOTA

WISCONSIN

ADDITIONAL INFORMATION:

Available Degree(s)

- BA in Fashion Studies, concentration: Product Development
- BFA in Fashion Design

Freshman Portfolio Requirement

BFA in Fashion Design

- 10-15 pieces
- Essay (300-500 words)
- Interview required, virtually or in-person

For more information, visit: https://www.colum.edu/admissions/additional-information/bfa-requirements

Portfolios are optional for all applications that apply to a BA program at Columbia College Chicago. Applicants are encouraged to submit a portfolio not only for admission to their desired program but also for the Faculty Recognition Award.

- Submit 10 annotated images in PDF format that demonstrate how you engage with fashion as a practice or industry
- May include drawings, product curation, color study work, materials investigation, styling, garments, digital media, etc.

For more information, visit: https://www.colum.edu/admissions/additional-information/portfolio-and-audition-requirements

Scholarships Offered
Applicants including international students are automatically considered for talent-based scholarships. A digital portfolio or audition is required. Many internal scholarships are awarded to local high school graduates. For more information, visit: https://www.colum.edu/columbia-central/scholarships/index

Special Opportunities
The Fashion Department hosts seminars every semester. Topics in the past have been on sustainability, diversity, and technology. The Digital Fashion Seminar has seen designers from Google, Levi's, Target, and other companies showcase wearable tech, 3D printing, and other technologically-enhanced experiences.

Notable Alumni

- Alexander Knox: Fashion Designer and finalist on *Project Runway* season 13.

DOMINICAN UNIVERSITY

Address: 7900 West Division Street, River Forest, IL 60305
Website: https://www.dom.edu/academics/majors-programs/
fashion-design
Contact: https://www.dom.edu/about-dominican/contact-us
Request for Information: https://www.dom.edu/admission/
request-information
Phone: (708) 366-2490
Email: domadmis@dom.edu

COST OF ATTENDANCE:

Tuition & Fees: $36,500 | **Additional Expenses:** $13,622
Total: $50,122

Financial Aid: https://www.dom.edu/admission/office-financial-aid

ADDITIONAL INFORMATION:

Available Degree(s)

- BA in Fashion Design

Freshman Portfolio Requirement

There is no portfolio requirement.

Scholarships Offered

Dominican University offers various scholarships, including the
Freshman Merit Scholarships based on academic performance,
which ranges from $10,000 to $20,000 annually. For more
information, visit: https://www.dom.edu/admission/scholarships-
dominican#undergraduate

Special Opportunities

Paris: Essentials of French Fashion is an exclusive study away
program for Fashion students which provides an immersed
experience from a French fashion perspective at the Paris American
Academy. Students can also spend a semester or a year at Milan's
Instituto di Moda Burgo or take a trip to New York City sponsored by
the Fashion department.

ILLINOIS

INDIANA

IOWA

KANSAS

MICHIGAN

MINNESOTA

MISSOURI

NEBRASKA

NORTH DAKOTA

OHIO

SOUTH DAKOTA

WISCONSIN

MIDWEST

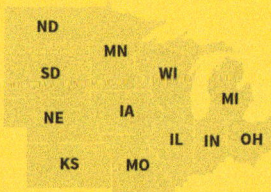

SCHOOL OF THE ART INSTITUTE OF CHICAGO (SAIC)

Address: 36 S. Wabash Ave., Chicago, IL 60603
Website: https://www.saic.edu/academics/departments/fashion-design
Contact: https://www.saic.edu/contact/
Request for Information: https://www.saic.edu/t4/request-information/
Phone: (312) 629-6101
Email: admiss@saic.edu

COST OF ATTENDANCE:

Tuition & Fees: $53,360 | **Additional Expenses:** $21,200
Total: $74,560

Financial Aid: https://www.saic.edu/financial-aid/

ADDITIONAL INFORMATION:

Available Degree(s)
- BFA in Fashion Design
- BFA in Fiber and Material Studies

Freshman Portfolio Requirement
The degree is a BFA in Studio. To get into the Fashion Design core, students must first complete their Contemporary Practices requirements and apply for admission to this concentration as a third-year undergraduate student.

- Submit via SlideRoom
- 10-15 pieces of best and most recent work
- Applicants may concentrate work in single media or show work in breadth of media
- Work may range from observational to abstract

For more information, visit: https://www.saic.edu/admissions/freshmen/how-to-apply

Scholarships Offered
SAIC offers Presidential, Distinguished, Honors, Recognition, Incentive, and Enrichment scholarships at varied amounts. These merit scholarships are based on the student's portfolio and application materials. In addition, students who participated in certain art exhibitions or competitions may be eligible for the Competitive Excellence Award ($2000).

Need-based scholarships are also available. Some of these include the John and Mary E. Hoggins Scholarship for female SAIC students, the Roger Brown and George Veronda Scholarship, or the LeRoy Neiman Scholarship. Award amounts vary. For more information on merit based and need-based scholarships, visit: https://www.saic.edu/financial-aid/saic-scholarships-and-grants

Special Opportunities
Students may specialize in an area of interest such as accessories, knitwear, etc. through the body-builder pathway. For more information, visit: https://www.saic.edu/academics/departments/fashion-design/undergraduate-overview

Notable Alumni
- Halston: Fashion Designer who was known for his minimal designs using cashmere or ultrasuede
- Cynthia Rowley: Fashion Designer based in New York City

ILLINOIS

INDIANA

IOWA

KANSAS

MICHIGAN

MINNESOTA

MISSOURI

NEBRASKA

NORTH DAKOTA

OHIO

SOUTH DAKOTA

WISCONSIN

INDIANA UNIVERSITY AT BLOOMINGTON

Address: 107 S. Indiana Avenue, Bloomington, IN 47405
Website: https://college.indiana.edu/academics/degrees-majors/
major-guides/fashion-design-ba.html
Contact: https://admissions.indiana.edu/contact/index.html
Request for Information: N/A
Phone: (812) 855-4848
Email: admissions@indiana.edu

COST OF ATTENDANCE:

In-State Tuition & Fees: $11,332 | **Additional Expenses:** $15,966
Total: $27,298

Out-of-State Tuition & Fees: $38,352 | **Additional Expenses:** $15,966
Total: $54,318

Financial Aid: https://admissions.indiana.edu/cost-financial-aid/
financial-aid.html

ADDITIONAL INFORMATION:

Available Degree(s)

- BA in Fashion Design

Freshman Portfolio Requirement

There is no portfolio requirement.

Scholarships Offered

Indiana University Bloomington offers a variety of scholarships
for in-state, out-of-state, and international students. Students
applying before the early action deadline will receive consideration
for IU Academic Scholarships ($1,000–$11,000) and for the
invitation-only Selective Scholarship. For more information,
visit: https://scholarships.indiana.edu/future-scholars/first-year-
scholarships.html

There are also scholarships offered at the College of Arts and
Sciences: https://theatre.indiana.edu/undergraduate/scholarships-
awards/index.html

Special Opportunities

High-achieving students may be eligible for Academic Excellence
within the College of Arts and Sciences or for admission to the
Hutton Honors College.

Previous fashion design students have interned at locations such as
Adidas/Reebok, Betsey Johnson, Express, Guess, Michael Kors, Saks
Fifth Avenue, and Ralph Lauren, among others.

Fashion design students often study abroad in study programs
at Wells College in Florence, Accademia Italiana, in Florence, or
London College of Fashion in England.

ILLINOIS

INDIANA

IOWA

KANSAS

MICHIGAN

MINNESOTA

MISSOURI

NEBRASKA

NORTH DAKOTA

OHIO

SOUTH DAKOTA

WISCONSIN

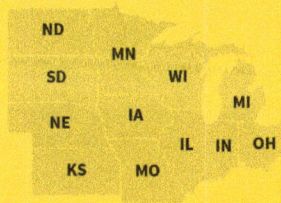

MIDWEST

ILLINOIS

INDIANA

IOWA

KANSAS

MICHIGAN

MINNESOTA

MISSOURI

NEBRASKA

NORTH DAKOTA

OHIO

SOUTH DAKOTA

WISCONSIN

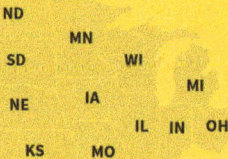

IOWA STATE UNIVERSITY

Address: 715 Bissell Rd, Ames, IA 50011
Website: https://www.hs.iastate.edu/find-majors/fashion_textiles/
Contact: https://www.admissions.iastate.edu/contact_us.php
Request for Information: https://www.admissions.iastate.edu/request_info.php
Phone: (515) 294-4111
Email: admissions@iastate.edu

COST OF ATTENDANCE:

In-State Tuition & Fees: $9,634 | **Additional Expenses:** $12,518
Total: $22,152

Out-of-State Tuition & Fees: $25,446 | **Additional Expenses:** $12,518
Total: $37,964

Financial Aid: https://www.financialaid.iastate.edu/

ADDITIONAL INFORMATION:

Available Degree(s)

- BS in Apparel, Merchandising, and Design, options:
  o Creative and Technical Design
  o Product Development and Innovation

Freshman Portfolio Requirement

There is no portfolio requirement.

Scholarships Offered

Iowa State offers merit-based awards to students of any major. These awards are based on GPA and ACT/SAT. Award amounts/criteria may vary from state to state. To review available awards by your State, visit: https://www.admissions.iastate.edu/scholarships/freshman.php

Special Opportunities

ISU houses numerous high-tech equipment, such as a 3D body scanner, an industrial digital printer, and state-of-the-art design software. Facilities include a textiles conservation laboratory, a historical garment collection, an apparel production center, and a clothing museum.

In addition to two classes on internships, careers, and professional opportunities, students enter ISU's highly acclaimed yearly Fashion Show. Fashion innovation classes incorporate textile and design thinking for unique markets and include accessories, non-apparel goods, and functional design. A merchandising certificate, minor in journalism focused on fashion influencing, accelerated degree program, and a concurrent bachelor's/master's degrees are also available.

Notable Alumni

- Todd Snyder: Menswear Fashion Design

KANSAS STATE UNIVERSITY

Address: 225 Justin Hall, 1324 Lovers Lane, Manhattan, KS 66506
Website: https://www.hhs.k-state.edu/idfs/fashion-studies/
Contact: https://www.k-state.edu/contact/
Request for Information: https://www.k-state.edu/admission/request-info/
Phone: (785) 532-6993
Email: idfsinfo@k-state.edu

COST OF ATTENDANCE:

In-State Tuition & Fees: $12,560 | **Additional Expenses:** $15,310
Total: $27,870

Out-of-State Tuition & Fees: $28,754 | **Additional Expenses:** $15,636
Total: $44,390

Financial Aid: https://www.k-state.edu/sfa/

ADDITIONAL INFORMATION:

Available Degree(s)

- BS in Fashion Studies, specialization: Fashion Design

Freshman Portfolio Requirement

There is no portfolio requirement.

Scholarships Offered

FASH Scholarships include awards gained via competitions through professional organizations. Some of these competitions include the Design-A-Throw Contest, the National Retail Federation Scholarships, and the Alpaca Owners Association Student Design Competition, among others. For more information, visit: https://www.hhs.k-state.edu/idfs/current-students/fashion-studies-scholarships/

Special Opportunities

All apparel and textiles students are required to participate in a 260-hour internship completed over Junior or Senior year. Internship locations in the past have included Gucci, J. Crew, Nordstrom, and Kohl's, among others. Students have worked in internships nationwide and internationally (UK, China, South Korea, India, and Nepal).

Students are encouraged to participate in study abroad on one of the regularly scheduled faculty-led study tours in Guatemala, Korea, Great Britain, Italy, and France. For more information, visit: https://www.hhs.k-state.edu/idfs/current-students/education-abroad.html

ILLINOIS

INDIANA

IOWA

KANSAS

MICHIGAN

MINNESOTA

MISSOURI

NEBRASKA

NORTH DAKOTA

OHIO

SOUTH DAKOTA

WISCONSIN

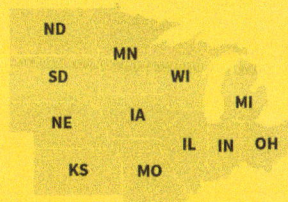

MIDWEST

ILLINOIS

INDIANA

IOWA

KANSAS

MICHIGAN

MINNESOTA

MISSOURI

NEBRASKA

NORTH DAKOTA

OHIO

SOUTH DAKOTA

WISCONSIN

MICHIGAN STATE UNIVERSITY

Address: Michigan State University, East Lansing, MI 48824
Website: https://art.msu.edu/undergraduate/apparel-textiles-ba-bfa/
Contact: https://admissions.msu.edu/contact-us/default.aspx
Request for Information: https://admissions.msu.edu/request-information
Phone: (517) 355-8332
Email: admis@msu.edu

COST OF ATTENDANCE:

In-State Tuition & Fees: $14,596 | **Additional Expenses:** $14,770
Total: $29,366

Out-of-State Tuition & Fees: $39,902 | **Additional Expenses:** $15,570
Total: $55,472

Financial Aid: https://admissions.msu.edu/cost-aid/need-based-aid/default.aspx

ADDITIONAL INFORMATION:

Available Degree(s)

- BA in Apparel & Textile Design
- BFA in Apparel & Textile Design

Freshman Portfolio Requirement

- Submit via MSU link
- Submit 10-15 artworks
- May include 2D work, 3D work, digital work, sewn garments, fashion illustrations, etc.

For more information, visit: https://art.msu.edu/undergraduate/portfolio-day/

Scholarships Offered

The College of Arts and Letters include departmental scholarships ranging from $1,200-$2,500 per year for four years. Portfolios may be used for consideration. For more information, visit: https://art.msu.edu/student-resources/scholarships-financial-aid/

Admitted students are automatically considered for scholarships. Students who apply by November 1 will receive the most scholarship consideration. There are scholarships specific to out-of-state residents, Michigan residents, high-achieving high school applicants, international residents, and criteria-specific scholarships. Awards go up to full tuition and fees for all four years. For more information, visit: https://admissions.msu.edu/cost-aid/merit-based-aid/freshman/default.aspx

Special Opportunities

MSU participates in Portfolio Day. Senior BFA students present a signature collection and craft a professional portfolio that reflects their career goals.

UNIVERSITY OF MINNESOTA

Address: 240 McNeal Hall, 1985 Buford Ave., St Paul, MN 55108
Website: https://apparel.design.umn.edu/
Contact: http://umn.force.com/admissions/
Request for Information: N/A
Phone: (612) 624-9700
Email: cdesinfo@umn.edu

COST OF ATTENDANCE:

In-State Tuition & Fees: $15,368 | **Additional Expenses:** $14,316
Total: $29,684

Out-of-State Tuition & Fees: $33,958 | **Additional Expenses:** $15,816
Total: $49,774

Financial Aid: https://admissions.tc.umn.edu/costsaid/index.html

ADDITIONAL INFORMATION:

Available Degree(s)

- BS in Apparel Design

Freshman Portfolio Requirement

There is no portfolio requirement.

Scholarships Offered

University of Minnesota offers numerous scholarship opportunities to all students, including in-state and out-of-state students. The University-Wide Academic Scholarships are highly competitive and have varying award amounts. In addition, all international students are automatically considered for the Global Excellence Scholarship ($10,000-$25,000 per year for up to four years). For more information, visit: https://admissions.tc.umn.edu/costsaid/scholarships.html

Students in the College of Design may be eligible for the Design, Housing, and Apparel Scholarship ($2,000-$3,000) or the Legacy Scholarship ($3,000 per year for four years). For more information, visit: https://admissions.tc.umn.edu/costsaid/schol_college.html#cdes

Special Opportunities

Students may study abroad in locations such as London, Florence, and Sydney. There are also short-term study tours to New York and other international locations.

Notable Alumni

- Juan Andrés Rujana: Design Director, Epimonia

ILLINOIS

INDIANA

IOWA

KANSAS

MICHIGAN

MINNESOTA

MISSOURI

NEBRASKA

NORTH DAKOTA

OHIO

SOUTH DAKOTA

WISCONSIN

MIDWEST

ILLINOIS

INDIANA

IOWA

KANSAS

MICHIGAN

MINNESOTA

MISSOURI

NEBRASKA

NORTH DAKOTA

OHIO

SOUTH DAKOTA

WISCONSIN

STEPHENS COLLEGE

Address: 1200 E Broadway, Columbia, MO 65215
Website: https://www.stephens.edu/academics/undergraduate-programs/fashion-design-product-development/
Contact: https://www.stephens.edu/campus-offices/
Request for Information: https://stephenscollege.secure.force.com/form?formid=217721
Phone: (573) 442-2211
Email: info@stephens.edu

COST OF ATTENDANCE:

Tuition & Fees: $23,385 | **Additional Expenses:** $12,864
Total: $36,249

Financial Aid: https://www.stephens.edu/admission-aid/undergraduate/financial-aid/

ADDITIONAL INFORMATION:

Available Degree(s)

- BA in Apparel Studies
- BFA in Fashion Design and Product Development

Freshman Portfolio Requirement

There is no portfolio requirement.

Scholarships Offered

Fashion students consistently receive scholarships through the Fashion Scholarship Fund and Fashion Group International.

Stephens College offers various institutional merit-based scholarships for incoming freshmen and transfer students. Rewards range from $1,000 to $8,000 and are typically renewable for four years. For more information, visit: https://www.stephens.edu/admission-aid/undergraduate/financial-aid/first-year-scholarships/

Special Opportunities

In the Jeannene Booher Fashion Lecture Series, Stephens College invites industry professionals to conduct a lecture series. In the past, guest lecturers have included Brandon Maxwell and Becca McCharen-Tran. For more information, visit: https://www.stephens.edu/academics/undergraduate-programs/jeannene-booher-fashion-lecture-series/

Notable Alumni

- Amy Bond: Competed in the 16th season of Project Runway
- Jeannene Booher: a partner and designer for the Maggy London dress company for ten years and owner of the Jeannene Booher Ltd.

WASHINGTON UNIVERSITY IN ST. LOUIS

Address: 1 Brookings Dr., St. Louis, MO 63130
Website: https://samfoxschool.wustl.edu/academics/college-of-art/bfa-ba-in-studio-art-and-design/fashion-design
Contact: https://admissions.wustl.edu/contact-us/
Request for Information: https://pathway.wustl.edu/register/request-information
Phone: (314) 935-5858
Email: admissions@wustl.edu

COST OF ATTENDANCE:

Tuition & Fees: $57,750 | **Additional Expenses:** $19,016
Total: $76,766

Financial Aid: https://financialaid.wustl.edu/

ADDITIONAL INFORMATION:

Available Degree(s)

- BFA in Fashion Design
- BA in Design, concentration: Fashion Design

Freshman Portfolio Requirement

- Submit via SlideRoom
- Submit 10-20 pieces of best and most recent work
- To be considered for the Conway/Proetz Scholarships in Art, the applicant must submit a digital portfolio via SlideRoom
- Majority of work should include finished works, however 2-3 sketches/quick drawings are accepted

For more information, visit: https://samfoxschool.wustl.edu/admissions/undergraduate/faq/

Scholarships Offered

Students may submit a digital portfolio to be considered for the Conway/Proetz Scholarships in Art.

WashU offers merit-based and need-based scholarships for students in any major. Some of these institutional scholarships cover the full cost of tuition. They also offer the Signature Scholar Program, which involves individual applications and a weekend program. Partial and full tuition are offered within this scholarship program. For more information, visit: https://financialaid.wustl.edu/how-aid-works/types-of-aid/scholarships/

Special Opportunities

Fashion students complete a capstone in their senior year. During this time, the student is guided by professional mentors and faculty throughout the design process and final construction. Senior works are featured in the annual WashU Fashion Design Show.

ILLINOIS

INDIANA

IOWA

KANSAS

MICHIGAN

MINNESOTA

MISSOURI

NEBRASKA

NORTH DAKOTA

OHIO

SOUTH DAKOTA

WISCONSIN

MIDWEST

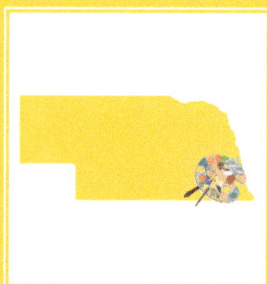

ILLINOIS

INDIANA

IOWA

KANSAS

MICHIGAN

MINNESOTA

MISSOURI

NEBRASKA

NORTH DAKOTA

OHIO

SOUTH DAKOTA

WISCONSIN

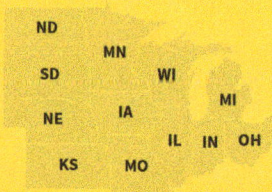

UNIVERSITY OF NEBRASKA

Address: 4th and R St, Lincoln, NE 68588
Website: https://cehs.unl.edu/tmfd/programs/textiles-fashion-design/
Contact: https://admissions.unl.edu/contact-us/
Request for Information: N/A
Phone: (402) 472-2023
Email: admissions@unl.edu

COST OF ATTENDANCE:

In-State Tuition & Fees: $7,770 | **Additional Expenses:** $14,242
Total: $22,012

Out-of-State Tuition & Fees: $24,900 | **Additional Expenses:** $14,242
Total: $39,142

Financial Aid: https://admissions.unl.edu/cost/#financial-aid

ADDITIONAL INFORMATION:

Available Degree(s)

- BS in Textiles & Apparel Design
- BS in Textiles, Merchandising, & Fashion Design/Communications
- BS in Textile Science

Freshman Portfolio Requirement

There is no portfolio requirement.

Scholarships Offered

First-year scholarships are merit-based and range from $1,000 to full tuition. There are also various financial opportunities for in-state and out-of-state students. For more information, visit: https://admissions.unl.edu/cost/

Special Opportunities

The Department of Textiles, Merchandising, and Fashion Design offers students international experiences such as the Annual Summer Sessions study tours and semesters abroad. Summer session study tours have previously been held in New York City, Europe (Paris, London, Prague, Milan), and Asia (Shanghai and Beijing). The semester abroad has been held in Lorenzo de' Medici, the Italian International Institute, the American Intercontinental University, and University of the Arts in London. For more information, visit: https://cehs.unl.edu/tmfd/study-tours/

COLUMBUS COLLEGE OF ART AND DESIGN

Address: 60 Cleveland Ave, Columbus, OH 43215
Website: https://www.ccad.edu/academics/fashion-design
Contact: https://www.ccad.edu/directory
Request for Information: https://www.ccad.edu/admissions/request-info
Phone: (614) 224-9101
Email: admissions@ccad.edu

COST OF ATTENDANCE:

Tuition & Fees: $37,370 | **Additional Expenses:** $17,208
Total: $54,578

Financial Aid: https://www.ccad.edu/admissions/financial-aid

ADDITIONAL INFORMATION:

Available Degree(s)

- BFA Fashion Design

Freshman Portfolio Requirement

- Submit via SlideRoom
- 8-15 works that showcase creative ideas and technical skills
- Students may request a one-on-one portfolio review prior to applying to obtain critical feedback

For more information on portfolio requirements, visit: https://www.ccad.edu/admissions/applying-ccad/preparing-your-portfolio

Scholarships Offered

CCAD offers academic and merit scholarships. There are also external scholarship opportunities, such as the Ohio Governor's Youth Art Exhibition, the Lounge Lizard scholarship competition, MVP Scholarships ($500) and more. For more information, visit: https://www.ccad.edu/admissions/financial-aid-and-tuition-info/ccad-scholarships

Special Opportunities

High school students in grades 10-12 may attend College Preview. Students select a program, attend classes, workshops, & activities, and earn 3 college credits. Program options include Animation, Comics & Narrative Practice, Fashion Design, Fine Arts, Illustration, and for students who cannot decide, CCAD offers 3 Multi-disciplinary tracks. For more information, visit: https://www.ccad.edu/college-preview

CCAD participates in National Portfolio Day. For more information, visit: https://www.ccad.edu/national-portfolio-day

ILLINOIS

INDIANA

IOWA

KANSAS

MICHIGAN

MINNESOTA

MISSOURI

NEBRASKA

NORTH DAKOTA

OHIO

SOUTH DAKOTA

WISCONSIN

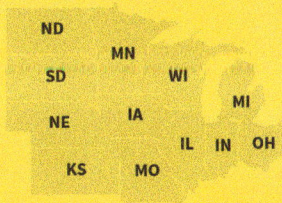

MIDWEST

ILLINOIS

INDIANA

IOWA

KANSAS

MICHIGAN

MINNESOTA

MISSOURI

NEBRASKA

NORTH DAKOTA

OHIO

SOUTH DAKOTA

WISCONSIN

KENT STATE UNIVERSITY

Address: 515 Hilltop Drive, Kent, OH 44242
Website: https://www.kent.edu/fashion/undergraduate-programs
Contact: https://www.kent.edu/theatredance/contact-us
Request for Information: https://ksu.secure.force.com/
form/?formid=217802
Phone: (330) 672-2082
Email: theatre@kent.edu

COST OF ATTENDANCE:

In-State Tuition & Fees: $11,923 | **Additional Expenses:** $17,745
Total: $29,668

Out-of-State Tuition & Fees: $20,799 | **Additional Expenses:** $17,745
Total: $38,544

Financial Aid: https://www.kent.edu/financialaid

ADDITIONAL INFORMATION:

Available Degree(s)

- BA in Fashion Design
- BFA in Fashion Design

Freshman Portfolio Requirement

There is no portfolio requirement. Students applying to any Fashion Design program must have at least a 3.0 cumulative GPA. Students who cannot meet these criteria will not be accepted into the programs but may be eligible to the pre-fashion design major. These students may declare a fashion design major after completing 12+ hours of college-level coursework at Kent State with a cumulative GPA of 2.75+.For more information, visit: https://www.kent.edu/admissions/first-year-student-requirements

Scholarships Offered

Both in-state and out-of-state applicants are eligible for merit-based awards, including the President's Achievement Award ($1,000 - $4,000 for in-state students and $4,000-$12,500 for out-of-state students), the Honors Distinction Award ($2,000), and the Founders Scholarship ($1,000-$2,000). For more information, visit: https://www.kent.edu/scholarships

Special Opportunities

Study away opportunities are available in "six European and Asian countries, two faculty-led study tours, various internship opportunities, and domestic study away experiences in New York and Los Angeles". For more information, visit: https://www.kent.edu/fashion/study-away

Every Match at the Cleveland Botanical Garden, Kent State participates in the Fashion Meets the Botanicals fashion show. This show is orchid-inspired and produced by junior design students. Students in this competition use an image of an orchid to create a computer-generated design from custom fabric. For more information, visit: https://www.kent.edu/fashion/fashion-meets-botanicals

UNIVERSITY OF CINCINNATI

Address: 2600 Clifton Ave, Cincinnati, OH 45221
Website: https://daap.uc.edu/academic-programs/school-of-design/fashion-design.html
Contact: https://admissions.uc.edu/contact.html
Request for Information: https://admissions.uc.edu/contact/request-info.html
Phone: (513) 556-1376
Email: daap-admissions@uc.edu

COST OF ATTENDANCE:

In-State Tuition & Fees: $12,598 | **Additional Expenses:** $16,510
Total: $29,108

Out-of-State Tuition & Fees: $27,932 | **Additional Expenses:** $11,874
Total: $44,442

Financial Aid: https://financialaid.uc.edu/

ADDITIONAL INFORMATION:

Available Degree(s)

- BSDES in Fashion Design

Freshman Portfolio Requirement

Portfolios are optional.

- Submit via link sent after completing Common App
- 12-20 pieces of recent work
- Include drawings from observation

For more information, visit: https://daap.uc.edu/academic-programs/school-of-design/fashion-design.html

Scholarships Offered

Applicants are automatically reviewed for merit-based scholarships at the University of Cincinnati. The University of Cincinnati Global Scholarship ($1,000 to $15,000 each year) is exclusively for international applicants. For more information, visit: https://www.kent.edu/scholarships

Special Opportunities

University of Cincinnati hosts the annual Design, Architecture, Art, and Planning (DAAP) Fashion Show and a VIP Pre-Show Reception. This is an opportunity for students to showcase their work. For more information, visit: https://daap.uc.edu/community/daap-fashion-show

Notable Alumni

- Tim Brown: Founder, Allbirds
- Stan Herman: Winner, Coty Fashion Critics Award, former President, Council of Fashion Designers of America, Lifetime Achievement Award winner

ILLINOIS

INDIANA

IOWA

KANSAS

MICHIGAN

MINNESOTA

MISSOURI

NEBRASKA

NORTH DAKOTA

OHIO

SOUTH DAKOTA

WISCONSIN

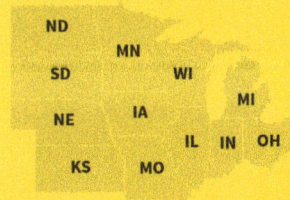

MIDWEST

ALABAMA

ARKANSAS

DELAWARE

DISTRICT OF COLUMBIA

FLORIDA

GEORGIA

KENTUCKY

LOUISIANA

MARYLAND

MISSISSIPPI

NORTH CAROLINA

OKLAHOMA

SOUTH CAROLINA

TENNESSEE

TEXAS

VIRGINIA

WEST VIRGINIA

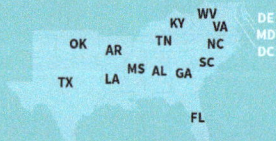

CHAPTER 16

REGION THREE

SOUTH

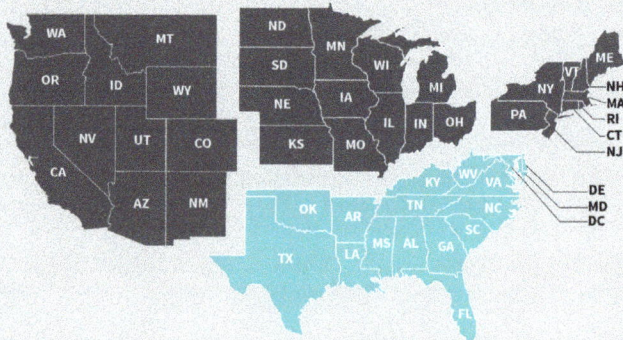

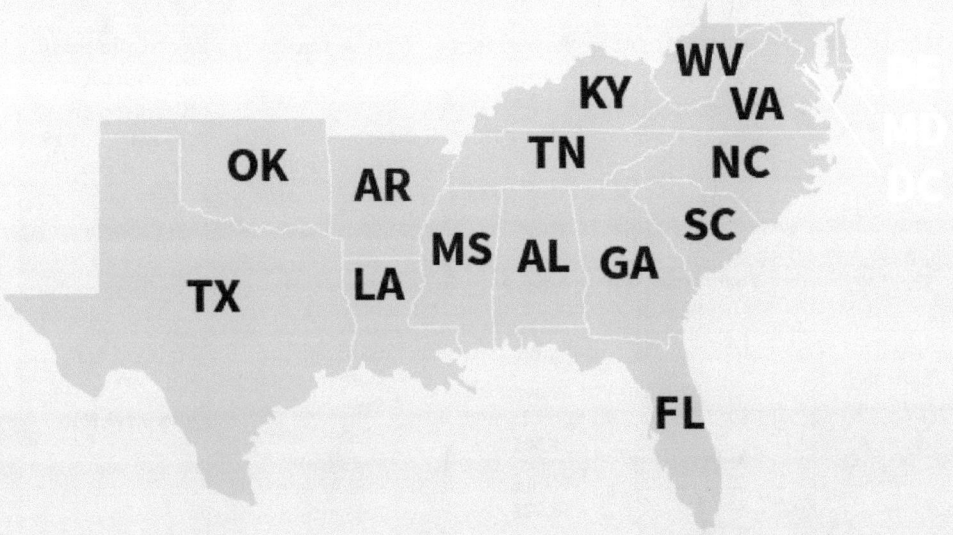

18 Programs | 16 States

1. AL - Auburn University
2. DE - Delaware State University
3. DE - University of Delaware
4. FL - Miami International University Art & Design
5. GA - Savannah College of Art & Design (SCAD)
6. LA - Louisiana State University (LSU)
7. MD - Maryland Institute College of Art (MICA)
8. NC - North Carolina State, Raleigh College of Design

9. NC - University of North Carolina at Greensboro
10. OK - Oklahoma State University
11. TX - Baylor University
12. TX - Texas Tech University
13. TX - Texas Woman's University
14. TX - University of North Texas
15. TX - University of Texas, Austin
16. TX - University of the Incarnate Word
17. VA - Virginia Commonwealth University
18. VA - Virginia Polytechnic Institute and State University (Virginia Tech)

FASHION DESIGN PROGRAMS

School	Avg. GPA, SAT Evidence-Based Reading Writing (ERW), SAT Math (M), and ACT Composite (C) Early Decision (ED): Yes/No	Admission Statistics	Program(s)	Portfolio and/or Interview Required (Req.)
Auburn University 210 Spidle Hall, Auburn, AL 36849	GPA: 3.97 SAT (ERW): 590-650 SAT (M): 570-670 ACT (C): 25-31 ED: No	Admit Rate: 85% Undergrad Enrollment: 24,505 Total Enrollment: 30,737 Program Completion (2020): 88	BS in Apparel Merchandising, Design, and Production Management, option: Apparel Design and Production Management	Portfolio: Not req. Interview: Not req.
Delaware State University 1200 N Dupont Hwy, Dover, DE 19901	GPA: N/A SAT (ERW): 420-520 SAT (M): 390-490 ACT (C): 17-22 ED: No	Admit Rate: 39% Undergrad Enrollment: 4,131 Total Enrollment: 4,739 Program Completion (2020): 2	BS in Textiles and Apparel Studies, concentration: Fashion Design	Portfolio: Not req. Interview: Not req.
University of Delaware 211 Alison Hall West, University of Delaware, Newark, DE 19716	GPA: 3.92 SAT (ERW): 580-660 SAT (M): 570-670 ACT (C): 25-30 ED: No	Admit Rate: 66% Undergrad Enrollment: 19,328 Total Enrollment: 23,613 Program Completion (2020): 10	BS in Fashion Design and Product Innovation	Portfolio: Optional Interview: Not req.

FASHION DESIGN PROGRAMS

School	Avg. GPA, SAT Evidence-Based Reading Writing (ERW), SAT Math (M), and ACT Composite (C) Early Decision (ED): Yes/No	Admission Statistics	Program(s)	Portfolio and/or Interview Required (Req.)
Miami International University Art & Design 1501 Biscayne Blvd Suite 100, Miami, FL 33132	GPA: N/A SAT (ERW): N/A SAT (M): N/A ACT (C): N/A *Miami International University Art & Design has an open admissions policy. ED: No	Admit Rate: N/A Undergrad Enrollment: 874 Total Enrollment: 934 Program Completion (2020): 8	BFA in Fashion Design	Portfolio: Not req. Interview: Not req.
Savannah College of Art & Design (SCAD) 342 Bull St., Savannah, GA 31401	GPA: 3.6 SAT (ERW): 540-640 SAT (M): 500-600 ACT (C): 20-27 ED: No	Admit Rate: 78% Undergrad Enrollment: 11,679 Total Enrollment: 14,265 Program Completion (2020): 162	BFA in Accessory Design BFA in Fashion BFA in Fibers	Portfolio: Optional Interview: Not req.
Louisiana State University (LSU) Louisiana State University, Baton Rouge, LA 70803	GPA: 3.45 SAT (ERW): 550-660 SAT (M): 540-640 ACT (C): 23-28 ED: No	Admit Rate: 73% Undergrad Enrollment: 27,825 Total Enrollment: 34,285 Program Completion (2020): 40	BS in Textiles, Apparel, & Merchandising, concentrations: Apparel Design Textile Science	Portfolio: Not req. Interview: Not req.

SOUTH

FASHION DESIGN PROGRAMS

School	Avg. GPA, SAT Evidence-Based Reading Writing (ERW), SAT Math (M), and ACT Composite (C) Early Decision (ED): Yes/No	Admission Statistics	Program(s)	Portfolio and/or Interview Required (Req.)
Maryland Institute College of Art (MICA) 1300 W. Mount Royal Ave., Baltimore, MD 21217	GPA: SAT (ERW): SAT (M): ACT (C): ED: Yes	Admit Rate: Undergrad Enrollment: Total Enrollment: Program Completion (2020): 17	BFA in Fiber, concentration: Experimental Fashion	Portfolio: Req. Interview: Not req.
North Carolina State University, Raleigh College of Design 1020 Main Campus Dr., Raleigh, NC 27606	GPA: 3.8 SAT (ERW): 620-690 SAT (M): 630-730 ACT (C): 27-32 ED: No	Admit Rate: 46% Undergrad Enrollment: 26,150 Total Enrollment: 36,042 Program Completion (2020): N/A	BS in Fashion and Textile Design	Portfolio: Req. Interview: Req.
University of North Carolina, Greensboro 210 Stone Building, PO Box 26170, Greensboro, NC 27402-6170	GPA: 3.67 SAT (ERW): 490-590 SAT (M): 490-570 ACT (C): 19-25 ED: No	Admit Rate: 88% Undergrad Enrollment: 15,995 Total Enrollment: 19,764 Program Completion (2020): 76	BS in Consumer, Apparel, and Retail Studies, concentration: Apparel Design	Portfolio: Not req. Interview: Not req.

FASHION DESIGN PROGRAMS

School	Avg. GPA, SAT Evidence-Based Reading Writing (ERW), SAT Math (M), and ACT Composite (C) Early Decision (ED): Yes/No	Admission Statistics	Program(s)	Portfolio and/or Interview Required (Req.)
Oklahoma State University 431 Nancy Randolph Davis, Oklahoma State University, Stillwater, OK 74078	GPA: 3.59 SAT (ERW): 540-640 SAT (M): 520-640 ACT (C): 22-28 ED: No	Admit Rate: 67% Undergrad Enrollment: 20,323 Total Enrollment: 24,535 Program Completion (2020): N/A	BS in Fashion Design and Production, options: Design Production	Portfolio: Not req. Interview: Not req.
Baylor University 1311 S 5th St, Waco, TX 76706	GPA: N/A SAT (ERW): 600-680 SAT (M): 590-680 ACT (C): 26-31 ED: Yes	Admit Rate: 68% Undergrad Enrollment: 14,399 Total Enrollment: 19,297 Program Completion (2020): 9	BS in Apparel Design and Product Development	Portfolio: Not req. Interview: Not req.
Texas Tech University 2500 Broadway Lubbock, TX 79409	GPA: 3.63 SAT (ERW): 540-620 SAT (M): 530-620 ACT (C): 22-27 ED: No	Admit Rate: 70% Undergrad Enrollment: 33,269 Total Enrollment: 40,322 Program Completion (2020): 13	BS in Apparel Design and Manufacturing	Portfolio: Not req. Interview: Not req.

SOUTH

FASHION DESIGN PROGRAMS

School	Avg. GPA, SAT Evidence-Based Reading Writing (ERW), SAT Math (M), and ACT Composite (C) Early Decision (ED): Yes/No	Admission Statistics	Program(s)	Portfolio and/ or Interview Required (Req.)
Texas Woman's University Old Main Building 415, P.O. Box 425529, Denton, TX 76204-5529	GPA: 3.17 SAT (ERW): 480-580 SAT (M): 460-560 ACT (C): 16-22 ED: No	Admit Rate: 94% Undergrad Enrollment: 10,664 Total Enrollment: 16,433 Program Completion (2020): 7	BA in Fashion Design BA in Fashion Design/BS in Fashion Merchandising BA in Fashion Design/BBS in Business Administration, Entrepreneurship emphasis BA in Fashion Design/BBA in Marketing	Portfolio: Not req. Interview: Not req.
University of North Texas Chilton Hall 331, 410 S. Avenue C, Denton, TX 76201	GPA: N/A SAT (ERW): 530-630 SAT (M): 520-610 ACT (C): ED: No	Admit Rate: 84% Undergrad Enrollment: 32,814 Total Enrollment: 40,953 Program Completion (2020): 35	BFA in Fashion Design	Portfolio: Not req. Interview: Not req.
University of Texas, Austin (UT Austin) 200 W 24th Street, Stop A2700, Austin, Texas 78712-1247	GPA: N/A SAT (ERW): 610-720 SAT (M): 600-750 ACT (C): 26-33 ED: No	Admit Rate: 32% Undergrad Enrollment: 40,048 Total Enrollment: 50,476 Program Completion (2020): 54	BS in Textile and Apparel, options: Apparel, Function, and Technical Design Textiles and Apparel Honors	Portfolio: Not req. Interview: Not req.

FASHION DESIGN PROGRAMS

School	Avg. GPA, SAT Evidence-Based Reading Writing (ERW), SAT Math (M), and ACT Composite (C) Early Decision (ED): Yes/No	Admission Statistics	Program(s)	Portfolio and/ or Interview Required (Req.)
University of the Incarnate Word 4301 Broadway, San Antonio, TX 78209	GPA: 3.56 SAT (ERW): 480-580 SAT (M): 470-560 ACT (C): 17-23 ED: No	Admit Rate: 97% Undergrad Enrollment: 5,081 Total Enrollment: 7,917 Program Completion (2020): 7	BS in Fashion Management, concentration: Apparel Production and Design	Portfolio: Not req. Interview: Not req.
Virginia Commonwealth University Virginia Commonwealth University, Richmond, VA 23284	GPA: 3.72 SAT (ERW): 540-640 SAT (M): 520-610 ACT (C): 21-28 ED: No	Admit Rate: 91% Undergrad Enrollment: 21,943 Total Enrollment: 29,070 Program Completion (2020): 75	BFA in Fashion, concentration: Fashion Design	Portfolio: Req. Interview: Not req.
Virginia Polytechnic Institute and State University (Virginia Tech) Virginia Polytechnic Institute and State University, Blacksburg, VA 24061	GPA: 3.96 SAT (ERW): 590-680 SAT (M): 580-690 ACT (C): 25-31 ED: Yes	Admit Rate: 66% Undergrad Enrollment: 30,020 Total Enrollment: 37,024 Program Completion (2020): 77	BS in Fashion Merchandising and Design, specialization: Apparel Design and Production	Portfolio: Not req. Interview: Not req.

SOUTH

ALABAMA

ARKANSAS

DELAWARE

DISTRICT OF COLUMBIA

FLORIDA

GEORGIA

KENTUCKY

LOUISIANA

MARYLAND

MISSISSIPPI

NORTH CAROLINA

OKLAHOMA

SOUTH CAROLINA

TENNESSEE

TEXAS

VIRGINIA

WEST VIRGINIA

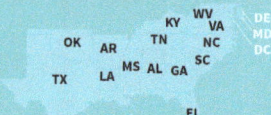

AUBURN UNIVERSITY

Address: 210 Spidle Hall, Auburn, AL 36849
Website: http://humsci.auburn.edu/apparel/index.php
Contact: http://www.auburn.edu/enrollment/contact_us.php
Request for Information: https://apply.auburn.edu/register/inquiryform
Phone: (334) 844-4084
Email: ulricpv@auburn.edu

COST OF ATTENDANCE:

In-State Tuition & Fees: $11,796 | **Additional Expenses:** $21,648
Total: $33,444

Out-of-State Tuition & Fees: $31,956 | **Additional Expenses:** $21,648
Total: $53,604

Financial Aid: http://www.auburn.edu/administration/business-finance/finaid/

ADDITIONAL INFORMATION:

Available Degree(s)

- BS in Apparel Merchandising, Design, and Production Management, option: Apparel Design and Production Management

Freshman Portfolio Requirement

There is no portfolio requirement.

Scholarships Offered

Merit-based and need-based aid available. Non-resident merit scholarships are up to $15,000 and resident merit scholarships go up to $8,000. For more information, visit: http://www.auburn.edu/scholarship/index.php#UndergraduateScholarships

Special Opportunities

"The Joseph S. Bruno Auburn Abroad in Italy program is strongly encouraged for apparel merchandising, design, and production management majors." The 12-week term is set in Ariccia, a small town near Rome. Students may earn their International Minor in Human Sciences while abroad. For more information, visit: http://www.humsci.auburn.edu/italy/index.php

Auburn's Apparel Design and Production Management concentrates on raw materials and manufactured products. With a consumer focus, Auburn's program is future-focused, emphasizing consumer preferences, market niches, and managing production. The program includes a team-based Apparel Line Development capstone course. Internships include domestic/international firms with couture designers or in industry and options for theatrical costuming, historical costumes, or textile collections.

Socially-conscious students may minor in Human Sciences (International), Hunger Studies, or Philanthropy and Non-Profit Studies.

Notable Alumni

- Lydia Pass: CEO, Stelona Shoes

DELAWARE STATE UNIVERSITY

Address: 1200 N Dupont Hwy, Dover, DE 19901
Website: https://cast.desu.edu/departments/human-ecology/
textiles-apparel-studies-bs
Contact: https://cast.desu.edu/about/contact-us
Request for Information: https://www.desu.edu/admissions/
request-info
Phone: (302) 857-6351
Email: admissions@desu.edu

COST OF ATTENDANCE:

In-State Tuition & Fees: $8,358 | **Additional Expenses:** $20,548
Total: $28,906

Out-of-State Tuition & Fees: $18,280 | **Additional Expenses:** $20,548
Total: $38,828

Financial Aid: https://www.desu.edu/admissions/financial-aid

ADDITIONAL INFORMATION:

Available Degree(s)

- BS in Textiles and Apparel Studies, concentration: Fashion Design

Freshman Portfolio Requirement

There is no portfolio requirement.

Scholarships Offered

There are numerous scholarship opportunities for all incoming students. Scholarships at DSU are merit-based and need-based. For more information, visit: https://www.desu.edu/admissions/
financial-aid/scholarships

Special Opportunities

Students may utilize a variety of facilities, such as the apparel construction laboratory, a textile testing lab, a computer-aided design center, the historic costume collection, and more. Furthermore, fashion students take field trips to major fashion centers, participate in design competitions, and obtain internships in the fashion industry.

ALABAMA

ARKANSAS

DELAWARE

DISTRICT OF COLUMBIA

FLORIDA

GEORGIA

KENTUCKY

LOUISIANA

MARYLAND

MISSISSIPPI

NORTH CAROLINA

OKLAHOMA

SOUTH CAROLINA

TENNESSEE

TEXAS

VIRGINIA

WEST VIRGINIA

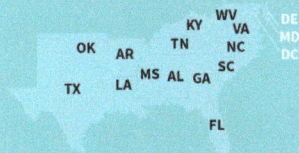

SOUTH

ALABAMA

ARKANSAS

DELAWARE

DISTRICT OF
COLUMBIA

FLORIDA

GEORGIA

KENTUCKY

LOUISIANA

MARYLAND

MISSISSIPPI

NORTH CAROLINA

OKLAHOMA

SOUTH CAROLINA

TENNESSEE

TEXAS

VIRGINIA

WEST VIRGINIA

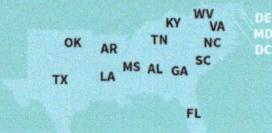

UNIVERSITY OF DELAWARE

Address: 211 Alison Hall West, University of Delaware, Newark, DE 19716
Website: https://www.fashion.udel.edu/undergraduate/majors-and-minors
Contact: https://www.fashion.udel.edu/about-us/contact-us
Request for Information: N/A
Phone: (302) 831-8714
Email: fashion-studies@udel.edu

COST OF ATTENDANCE:

In-State Tuition & Fees: $14,948 | **Additional Expenses:** $17,542
Total: $32,490

Out-of-State Tuition & Fees: $36,880 | **Additional Expenses:** $17,562
Total: $54,442

Financial Aid: https://www.udel.edu/students/student-financial-services/

ADDITIONAL INFORMATION:

Available Degree(s)

- BS in Fashion Design and Product Innovation

Freshman Portfolio Requirement

Portfolios are optional.

- Upload a portfolio or link to an online portfolio (Submit via Blue Hen Home Portal)
- Maximum 5 artifacts/examples of creative work
- Applicants may submit: garments, accessories, illustrations, etc.

For more information, visit: https://www.fashion.udel.edu/prospective-students/bachelor-of-science-in-fashion-design-and-product-innovation/fashion-design-and-innovation-portfolio-information

Scholarships Offered

Merit scholarships, need-based grants, and endowed scholarships are available at UDel. For more information, visit: https://www.udel.edu/apply/undergraduate-admissions/financing-your-degree/

Special Opportunities

Students are encouraged to study abroad. University of Delaware has opportunities for students to travel with faculty for one month during the winter session. Past locations have included Hong Kong (Internship), Paris, and Italy. Students may also travel domestically in the form of short field trips in New York City, Philadelphia, Washington, D.C., and California. For more information, visit: https://www.fashion.udel.edu/undergraduate/study-abroad-programs

Notable Alumni

- Dani Civil: Technical Designer, Under Armor
- Charquetta Hudson: The SEWcial Café, won award from True Access Capital
- Bai Li: Exoskeletal garment designer, NSF grant

MIAMI INTERNATIONAL UNIVERSITY OF ART & DESIGN

Address: 1501 Biscayne Blvd Suite 100, Miami, FL 33132
Website: https://www.artinstitutes.edu/miami/academics/fashion/fashion-design-degree-programs
Contact: https://www.artinstitutes.edu/miami/about/contact-us
Request for Information: https://www.artinstitutes.edu/miami/request-information
Phone: (800) 225-9023
Email: miuadmissions@aii.edu

COST OF ATTENDANCE:

Tuition & Fees: $17,698 | **Additional Expenses:** $13,998
Total: $31,696

Financial Aid: https://www.artinstitutes.edu/miami/tuition-aid/financial-aid

ADDITIONAL INFORMATION:

Available Degree(s)

- BFA in Fashion Design

Freshman Portfolio Requirement

There is no portfolio requirement.

Scholarships Offered

The Arts Institutes offers scholarships via competitions. Awards include the $1,000-$12,000 through the FCCLA Competitions, $1,000-$7,500 through the DECA Scholarship, 50% of the program total through the High School Initiative Scholarship, and more. For more information, visit: https://www.artinstitutes.edu/miami/tuition-aid/scholarships

Special Opportunities

Students study topics such as sketching/illustration, pattern-making and draping, computer-aided design, clothing design, and garment construction.

As creatives, entering the fashion world, students work in the collaborative space of fashion production and fashion showcases. Students study fashion history and fashion show production, pushing the boundaries to use unusual materials, solve problems in the fashion industry, and think outside of the box.

Students interested in Accessory Design can focus on hats, shoes, jewelry, handbags, and belts that complete outfits. Focuses include technical/fashion drawing, concept/product development, and merchandise management.

ALABAMA

ARKANSAS

DELAWARE

DISTRICT OF COLUMBIA

FLORIDA

GEORGIA

KENTUCKY

LOUISIANA

MARYLAND

MISSISSIPPI

NORTH CAROLINA

OKLAHOMA

SOUTH CAROLINA

TENNESSEE

TEXAS

VIRGINIA

WEST VIRGINIA

SOUTH

ALABAMA

ARKANSAS

DELAWARE

DISTRICT OF
COLUMBIA

FLORIDA

GEORGIA

KENTUCKY

LOUISIANA

MARYLAND

MISSISSIPPI

NORTH CAROLINA

OKLAHOMA

SOUTH CAROLINA

TENNESSEE

TEXAS

VIRGINIA

WEST VIRGINIA

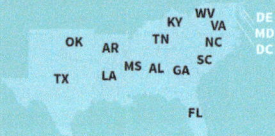

SAVANNAH COLLEGE OF ART & DESIGN (SCAD)

Address: 342 Bull St., Savannah, GA 31401
Website: https://www.scad.edu/academics/programs/fashion
Contact: https://www.scad.edu/about/contact
Request for Information: https://admission.scad.edu/forms/reqInfo/rfi2
Phone: (912) 525-5100
Email: contact@scad.edu
Other locations: Atlanta, GA

COST OF ATTENDANCE:

Tuition & Fees: $38,340 | **Additional Expenses:** $15,269
Total: $53,609

Financial Aid: https://www.scad.edu/admission/financial-aid-and-scholarships

ADDITIONAL INFORMATION:

Available Degree(s)
- BFA in Accessory Design
- BFA in Fashion
- BFA in Fibers

Freshman Portfolio Requirement
Portfolios are optional. However, they are required for achievement honors scholarship consideration.
- Submit via SlideRoom. All work submitted must be original in concept and fabrication
- Portfolio Applicants are encouraged to submit a portfolio related to their major of choice, though they may fall under any of the categories: Business and Marketing, Visual Arts, Time-based Media, Visual and Time-based Media, Writing, or Performing Arts
- For visual arts portfolios, applicants must submit 10-20 visual artworks and/or 3D renderings.

For more information, visit: https://www.scad.edu/admission/portfolio-and-writing-guidelines/undergraduate-portfolios

Scholarships Offered
SCAD offers two full tuition scholarships: The May and Paul Poetter Scholarship and the Frances Larkin McCommon Scholarship, both based on superior academic and/or artistic achievement. For more information, visit: https://www.scad.edu/admission/financial-aid-and-scholarships/scholarships/entering-students

Students may receive a scholarship award via the SCAD Challenge Scholarship. Awards range from $2,000-$4,000. For more information on this challenge, visit: https://www.scad.edu/admission/financial-aid-and-scholarships/scholarships/scad-challenge

Special Opportunities
GRADpath@SCAD offers incoming freshmen the opportunity to earn their undergraduate and graduate degrees in a continuous program of study. Students may complete a BFA and MA in four years or a BFA and MFA in five years. For more information, visit: https://www.scad.edu/admission/admission-information/freshman/gradpath

SCAD hosts a variety of style authorities each year. Students may participate in workshops, panel discussions, master classes, and critiques with the guest artists. Recent guests include: Alexander Wang, Betsey Johnson, Calvin Klein, Brandon Maxwell, Zac Posen, Vera Wang, and Oscar de la Renta among many others. For more information, visit: https://www.scad.edu/academics/programs/fashion/student-experience

LOUISIANA STATE UNIVERSITY (LSU)

Address: Louisiana State University, Baton Rouge, LA 70803
Website: https://www.lsu.edu/tam/
Contact: https://lsu.edu/about/requestinfo.php
Request for Information: https://www.lsu.edu/about/requestinfo.php
Phone: (225) 578-1175
Email: admissions@lsu.edu

COST OF ATTENDANCE:

In-State Tuition & Fees: $11,962 | **Additional Expenses:** $23,088
Total: $35,050

Out-of-State Tuition & Fees: $28,639 | **Additional Expenses:** $23,088
Total: $51,727

Financial Aid: https://www.lsu.edu/financialaid/index.php

ADDITIONAL INFORMATION:

Available Degree(s)

- BS in Textiles, Apparel, & Merchandising, concentrations:
  o Apparel Design
  o Textile Science

Freshman Portfolio Requirement

There is no portfolio requirement.

Scholarships Offered

Awards at LSU range from $500 to the full cost of attendance. The university offers merit-based scholarships, need-based awards, major-specific scholarships, the Stamps Scholarship, and several other types of opportunities for aid. For more information, visit: https://www.lsu.edu/financialaid/types_of_scholarships/entering_freshman_scholarships/index.php

Special Opportunities

The Department of Textiles, Apparel Design, and Merchandising houses numerous facilities for students to use, including but not limited to a sewing lab, 3D printing machine, apparel production lab, body scanning technology, a textile printer, and a textile science lab. For more information, visit: https://www.lsu.edu/tam/resources/facilities/

Notable Alumni

- Chelsey Blankenship & Annie Claire Bass: Founders, SoSis Boutique
- Madi Meserole: Owner womenswear label, MEZ Atelier
- Natasha Miller Popich: Owner, Natasha Marie Bridal
- Suzanne St. Paul: Celebrity Designer

ALABAMA
ARKANSAS
DELAWARE
DISTRICT OF COLUMBIA
FLORIDA
GEORGIA
KENTUCKY
LOUISIANA
MARYLAND
MISSISSIPPI
NORTH CAROLINA
OKLAHOMA
SOUTH CAROLINA
TENNESSEE
TEXAS
VIRGINIA
WEST VIRGINIA

SOUTH

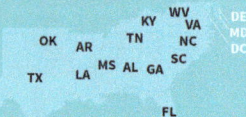

MARYLAND INSTITUTE COLLEGE OF ART (MICA)

Address: 1300 W. Mount Royal Ave., Baltimore, MD 21217
Website: https://www.mica.edu/undergraduate-majors-minors/fiber-major/
Contact: https://www.mica.edu/mica-dna/contact-us/
Request for Information: https://www.mica.edu/applying-to-mica/apply/request-more-information/
Phone: (410) 669-9200
Email: https://www.mica.edu/forms/contact-undergraduate-admission/

COST OF ATTENDANCE:

Tuition & Fees: $53,333 | **Additional Expenses:** $17,820
Total: $71,153

Financial Aid: https://www.mica.edu/financial-aid/

ADDITIONAL INFORMATION:

Available Degree(s)
- BFA in Fiber, concentration: Experimental Fashion

Freshman Portfolio Requirement
- Follow instructions in Common App for submission
- 12-20 of best and most recent work
- Strongly suggested that some direct observation drawings are included
- MICA recommends that students have experience and training in art by enrolling in art classes in high school over 2-3 years, pre-college programs, AP/IB art classes, or private art lessons

For more information, visit: https://www.mica.edu/applying-to-mica/apply/portfolio-preparation/portfolio-prep-for-freshman/

Scholarships Offered
MICA offers several, competitive merit-based scholarships to all incoming undergraduate students. Some of these offers include the Mathias J. Devito Scholarship Program ($40,000 over 4 years), the Fanny B. Thalheimer Scholarship ($16,000-$68,000 over four years), the Academic Excellence Scholarships ($12,000-$24,000) and several others. For more information, visit: https://www.mica.edu/financial-aid/undergraduate-financial-aid/new-students/financing-options/scholarships/competitive-scholarships/

Special Opportunities
The Fiber Arts Center houses studios, a dyeing facility, and seminar rooms. There are industrial and household sewing machines, sergers, computerized embroidery machines, floor looms, a steam cabinet, and other equipment for students to use. Students also have access to a 3D fabrication lab and a Smart Textiles Lab.

The Baltimore Natural Dye Initiative expands the curriculum related to utilizing natural dye. Two courses aim to engage artists and deepen the knowledge of using natural dyes in the Baltimore region. Both MICA and non-MICA students are in these courses. For more information, visit: https://www.mica.edu/annual-events-series/natural-dye-initiative/learning-about-natural-dye/

MICA participates in National Portfolio Day. In addition, portfolio preparation is available to high school sophomores and juniors during the summer Pre-College Studio Residency Programs. This program involves 2-week to 5-week studio courses. For more information, visit: https://www.mica.edu/non-degree-learning-opportunities/programs-for-youth/programs-for-teens/summer-pre-college-program/

ALABAMA

ARKANSAS

DELAWARE

DISTRICT OF COLUMBIA

FLORIDA

GEORGIA

KENTUCKY

LOUISIANA

MARYLAND

MISSISSIPPI

NORTH CAROLINA

OKLAHOMA

SOUTH CAROLINA

TENNESSEE

TEXAS

VIRGINIA

WEST VIRGINIA

NORTH CAROLINA STATE UNIVERSITY AT RALEIGH

Address: 1020 Main Campus Dr., Raleigh, NC 27606
Website: https://textiles.ncsu.edu/tatm/fashion-and-textile-design/
Contact: https://textiles.ncsu.edu/directory/people?group=textile-and-apparel-technology-and-management&compact=false
Request for Information: N/A
Phone: (919) 515-3442
Email: undergrad-admissions@ncsu.edu

COST OF ATTENDANCE:

In-State Tuition & Fees: $9,130 | **Additional Expenses:** $15,855
Total: $24,985

Out-of-State Tuition & Fees: $29,916 | **Additional Expenses:** $16,064
Total: $45,980

Financial Aid: https://studentservices.ncsu.edu/your-money/financial-aid/

ADDITIONAL INFORMATION:

Available Degree(s)

- BS in Fashion and Textile Design

Freshman Portfolio Requirement

- Interview required
- Submit via SlideRoom
- 10 images of most creative work
- Encouraged to include fashion/textile pieces if possible
- Videos and music not accepted
- 500-word essay required

For more information, visit: https://textiles.ncsu.edu/tatm/fashion-and-textile-design/

Scholarships Offered

The Fields Family Prestige Scholarship and the Jacques Weber International Scholarship offer varying award amounts for fashion and textile students. For more information, visit: https://studentservices.ncsu.edu/your-money/financial-aid/types/scholarships/

Special Opportunities

Students are encouraged to study abroad during their junior year. Destinations include France, the Czech Republic, Australia, China, and Italy.

Graduating seniors debut their work to hundreds in the FTD Emerging Designers Showcase.

ALABAMA

ARKANSAS

DELAWARE

DISTRICT OF COLUMBIA

FLORIDA

GEORGIA

KENTUCKY

LOUISIANA

MARYLAND

MISSISSIPPI

NORTH CAROLINA

OKLAHOMA

SOUTH CAROLINA

TENNESSEE

TEXAS

VIRGINIA

WEST VIRGINIA

SOUTH

ALABAMA

ARKANSAS

DELAWARE

DISTRICT OF
COLUMBIA

FLORIDA

GEORGIA

KENTUCKY

LOUISIANA

MARYLAND

MISSISSIPPI

NORTH CAROLINA

OKLAHOMA

SOUTH CAROLINA

TENNESSEE

TEXAS

VIRGINIA

WEST VIRGINIA

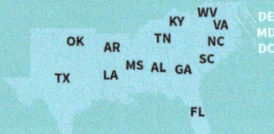

UNIVERSITY OF NORTH CAROLINA AT GREENSBORO

Address: 1400 Spring Garden St, Greensboro, NC 27402
Website: https://bryan.uncg.edu/department/consumer-apparel-and-retail-studies/
Contact: https://bryan.uncg.edu/contact/
Request for Information: https://spartanlink.uncg.edu/register.asp
Phone: (336) 334-5000
Email: admissions@uncg.edu

COST OF ATTENDANCE:

In-State Tuition & Fees: $7,406 | **Additional Expenses:** $9,423
Total: $16,829

Out-of-State Tuition & Fees: $22,565 | **Additional Expenses:** $9,423
Total: $31,988

Financial Aid: https://admissions.uncg.edu/costs-aid/costs/

ADDITIONAL INFORMATION:

Available Degree(s)

- BS in Consumer, Apparel, and Retail Studies, concentration: Apparel Design

Freshman Portfolio Requirement

There is no portfolio requirement.

Scholarships Offered

UNCG offers incoming freshmen merit-based scholarships. The Blue and Gold Scholarships range in value and may go up to the full cost of attendance. Students must submit a 250- to 500-word essay in addition to their application. Students may also be eligible for the need-based and merit-based Chancellor, Deans, and Spartan Awards. For more information on these opportunities and others, visit: https://admissions.uncg.edu/costs-aid/scholarships/

Special Opportunities

UNCG offers an Accelerated Master's Program (AMP) where students take graduate courses while enrolled as an undergraduate. AMP students may earn their graduate degree in 12-18 months after receiving their undergraduate degree. Eligible students include undergraduates who are currently pursuing the BS in CARS and meet certain academic criteria. For more information, visit: https://bryan.uncg.edu/programs/masters/list/consumer-apparel-and-retail-studies-accelerated-masters-program/

UNCG offers CARS students the chance to intern at various leading firms in the industry. Previous students who have interned at Polo/Ralph Lauren, VF Corporation and HanesBrands. Students may also intern in other cities such as New York or Los Angeles or internationally in places such as London or Hong Kong. These CARS students have interned at Tommy Hilfiger, Sak's 5th Avenue, and Calvin Klein.

OKLAHOMA STATE UNIVERSITY

Address: Oklahoma State University, Stillwater, OK 74078
Website: https://go.okstate.edu/undergraduate-academics/majors/fashion-design-and-production.html
Contact: https://go.okstate.edu/admissions/contact-us.html
Request for Information: N/A
Phone: (405) 744-5358
Email: admissions@okstate.edu

COST OF ATTENDANCE:

In-State Tuition & Fees: $13,920 | **Additional Expenses:** $11,000
Total: $24,920

Out-of-State Tuition & Fees: $29,440 | **Additional Expenses:** $11,000
Total: $40,440

Financial Aid: https://go.okstate.edu/scholarships-financial-aid/

ADDITIONAL INFORMATION:

Available Degree(s)

- BS in Fashion Design and Production, options:
  o Design
  o Production

Freshman Portfolio Requirement

There is no portfolio requirement.

Scholarships Offered

Students are automatically considered for scholarships when they apply for admission. Most scholarships are merit-based. There are a variety of in-state and out-of-state scholarships. Awards vary from $2,000 per year (based on GPA and ACT/SAT) to partnered scholarships that may cover full tuition for five years (National Merit Scholarship). For more information, visit: https://go.okstate.edu/scholarships-financial-aid/types-of-aid/scholarships-and-grants/freshman-scholarships/index.html

Special Opportunities

Students may attend the annual trip to New York where they meet alumni and interview at prospective internship locations. Additionally, there are faculty-led study abroad summer experiences where students may earn course credit in locations such as Paris, Spain, and London.

ALABAMA
ARKANSAS
DELAWARE
DISTRICT OF COLUMBIA
FLORIDA
GEORGIA
KENTUCKY
LOUISIANA
MARYLAND
MISSISSIPPI
NORTH CAROLINA
OKLAHOMA
SOUTH CAROLINA
TENNESSEE
TEXAS
VIRGINIA
WEST VIRGINIA

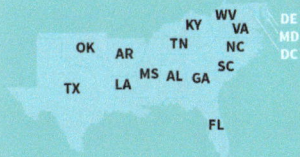

SOUTH

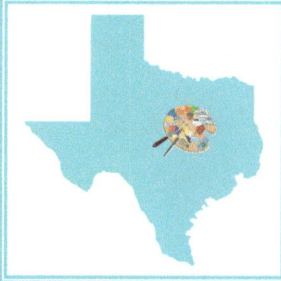

ALABAMA

ARKANSAS

DELAWARE

DISTRICT OF
COLUMBIA

FLORIDA

GEORGIA

KENTUCKY

LOUISIANA

MARYLAND

MISSISSIPPI

NORTH CAROLINA

OKLAHOMA

SOUTH CAROLINA

TENNESSEE

TEXAS

VIRGINIA

WEST VIRGINIA

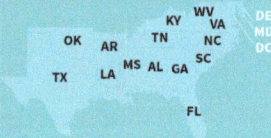

BAYLOR UNIVERSITY

Address: 1311 S 5th St, Waco, TX 76706
Website: https://www.baylor.edu/hsd/index.php?id=937885
Contact: https://www.baylor.edu/admissions/index.php?id=871966
Request for Information: N/A
Phone: (254) 710-3436
Email: admissions@baylor.edu

COST OF ATTENDANCE:

Tuition & Fees: $50,232 | **Additional Expenses:** $12,682
Total: $62,914

Financial Aid: https://www.baylor.edu/admissions/index.php?id=871964

ADDITIONAL INFORMATION:

Available Degree(s)

- BS in Apparel Design and Product Development

Freshman Portfolio Requirement

There is no portfolio requirement.

Scholarships Offered

The Family & Consumer Sciences Department offers scholarships to current undergraduates. All of these scholarships are based on merit, and some are also need-based. Seniors or Junior Apparel Design majors may be eligible for the Apparel Design/Product Development Scholarship. For more information, visit: https://www.baylor.edu/fcs/index.php?id=947273

According to Baylor, 86% of applicants receive an academic scholarship. The median range awarded is $64,000 over four years. All applicants are considered for an academic scholarship, even if they apply as test optional. In addition, students in the Honors College may have additional scholarship opportunities. For more information, visit: https://www.baylor.edu/admissions/index.php?id=872109

Special Opportunities

Students must complete an internship as part of their degree requirements. Previous students have interned in New York, Paris, London, Los Angeles, Dallas, and many other locations.

Additionally, students plan the departmental fashion show and oversee public relations, ticket sales, training of models, and more. Student designer showcase their work during this fashion show. For more information, visit: https://www.baylor.edu/fcs/index.php?id=950321

Apparel studies students can take an immersive learning experience in the major three European fashion capitals of London, Paris and Florence/Milan with weekday lectures, professional visits, and opportunities to obtain an in-depth understanding of fashion industry.

TEXAS TECH UNIVERSITY

Address: 2500 Broadway Lubbock, TX 79409
Website: https://www.depts.ttu.edu/hs/prospective_students/
fashion/apparel_design.php
Contact: https://www.ttu.edu/about/contact.php
Request for Information: Press "Request More Information" -
https://www.depts.ttu.edu/hs/prospective_students/fashion/
apparel_design.php
Phone: (806) 742-2011
Email: admissions@ttu.edu

COST OF ATTENDANCE:

In-State Tuition & Fees: $11,600 | **Additional Expenses:** $15,556
Total: $27,156

Out-of-State Tuition & Fees: $23,870 | **Additional Expenses:** $15,556
Total: $39,426

Financial Aid: http://www.depts.ttu.edu/financialaid/

ADDITIONAL INFORMATION:

Available Degree(s)

- BS in Apparel Design and Manufacturing

Freshman Portfolio Requirement

There is no portfolio requirement.

Scholarships Offered

Students who apply test-optional may still be eligible for merit
scholarships and will be evaluated holistically. TTU's Presidential
Merit Scholarships range in value from $1,000-$8,500 per year.
Additionally, National Merit Finalists may receive $26,000+
per year. For more information, visit: http://www.depts.ttu.
edu/scholarships/

Special Opportunities

TECHstyle is a chance for students to show off their work. Hosted
by the Department of Design, Apparel Design and Manufacturing
(ADM) students showcase student collections and portfolios for
public viewing.

Additionally, ADM students can participate in the design
competitions that are held throughout the academic year. Junior
and senior-level students enrolled in a particular course are
required to participate in the Dallas Career Day Fashion Design
Competition. The students have faculty supervision. For more
information, visit: https://www.depts.ttu.edu/hs/dod/adm/
competitions.php

ALABAMA

ARKANSAS

DELAWARE

**DISTRICT OF
COLUMBIA**

FLORIDA

GEORGIA

KENTUCKY

LOUISIANA

MARYLAND

MISSISSIPPI

NORTH CAROLINA

OKLAHOMA

SOUTH CAROLINA

TENNESSEE

TEXAS

VIRGINIA

WEST VIRGINIA

SOUTH

ALABAMA

ARKANSAS

DELAWARE

DISTRICT OF
COLUMBIA

FLORIDA

GEORGIA

KENTUCKY

LOUISIANA

MARYLAND

MISSISSIPPI

NORTH CAROLINA

OKLAHOMA

SOUTH CAROLINA

TENNESSEE

TEXAS

VIRGINIA

WEST VIRGINIA

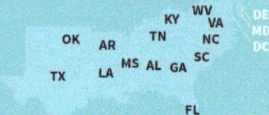

TEXAS WOMAN'S UNIVERSITY

Address: 304 Administration Dr, Denton, TX 76204
Website: https://twu.edu/fashion/
Contact: https://twu.edu/contact-twu/
Request for Information: https://twu.edu/admissions/info-request/
Phone: (866) 809-6130
Email: admissions@twu.edu

COST OF ATTENDANCE:

In-State Tuition & Fees: $9,960 | **Additional Expenses:** $14,586
Total: $24,546

Out-of-State Tuition & Fees: $22,230 | **Additional Expenses:** $14,586
Total: $36,816

Financial Aid: https://twu.edu/finaid/

ADDITIONAL INFORMATION:

Available Degree(s)

- BA in Fashion Design
- BA in Fashion Design/BS in Fashion Merchandising
- BA in Fashion Design/BBS in Business Administration, Entrepreneurship emphasis
- BA in Fashion Design/BBA in Marketing

Freshman Portfolio Requirement

There is no portfolio requirement.

Scholarships Offered

TWU offers many scholarship opportunities for freshmen and transfer students. Scholarships are need-based and/or merit-based and vary in award amounts. Additionally, fashion students may be eligible for Fashion and Textiles scholarships. Students must apply separately to these awards. For more information, visit: https://twu.edu/fashion/scholarships/

Special Opportunities

TWU fashion students have interned at places such as Aaron Browther, Aldo, Betsey Johnson, JC Penney, and more. Furthermore, students may work in TWU's new sewing lab, the advanced design lab with industrial sewing machines, the fashion sketching lab, and other facilities.

UNIVERSITY OF NORTH TEXAS

Address: 1201 W. Mulberry St., Denton, TX 76201
Website: https://cvad.unt.edu/design/fashion-design-bfa
Contact: https://admissions.unt.edu/contact-us
Request for Information: https://admissions.unt.edu/requestinfo
Phone: (940) 565-2855
Email: cvad@unt.edu

COST OF ATTENDANCE:

In-State Tuition & Fees: $11,514 | **Additional Expenses:** $13,860
Total: $25,374

Out-of-State Tuition & Fees: $24,514 | **Additional Expenses:** $13,860
Total: $38,374

Financial Aid: https://financialaid.unt.edu/

ADDITIONAL INFORMATION:

Available Degree(s)

- BFA in Fashion Design

Freshman Portfolio Requirement

There is no portfolio requirement.

Scholarships Offered

The College of Visual Arts and Design awards scholarships to eligible students. In addition, University of North Texas offers institutional aid to all students. Some merit-based awards include the UNT Excellence Scholarship ($1,000-$10,000), the UNT Meritorious Scholarship for National Merit Finalists (full cost of attendance), among others. For more information, visit: https://financialaid.unt.edu/types-scholarships

Special Opportunities

Students have access to the Texas Fashion Collection, housing over 18,000 articles of historic clothing and accessories. For more information, visit: https://art.unt.edu/design/fashion-design/texas-fashion-collection

Notable Alumni

- Shirin Askari: a contestant on *Project Runway* in the show's 6th season
- Heather Amuny Dey: Creative Director for the Nike Global Brand
- Victoria Bleakly: Technical Designer for The Row

ALABAMA
ARKANSAS
DELAWARE
DISTRICT OF COLUMBIA
FLORIDA
GEORGIA
KENTUCKY
LOUISIANA
MARYLAND
MISSISSIPPI
NORTH CAROLINA
OKLAHOMA
SOUTH CAROLINA
TENNESSEE
TEXAS
VIRGINIA
WEST VIRGINIA

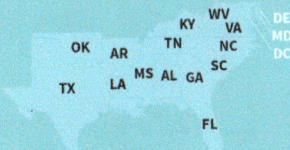

SOUTH

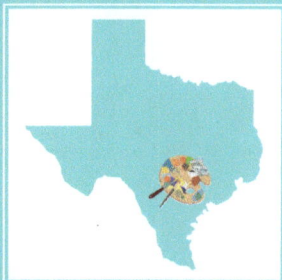

ALABAMA

ARKANSAS

DELAWARE

DISTRICT OF COLUMBIA

FLORIDA

GEORGIA

KENTUCKY

LOUISIANA

MARYLAND

MISSISSIPPI

NORTH CAROLINA

OKLAHOMA

SOUTH CAROLINA

TENNESSEE

TEXAS

VIRGINIA

WEST VIRGINIA

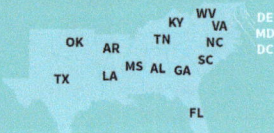

UNIVERSITY OF TEXAS, AUSTIN (UT AUSTIN)

Address: UT Austin, Austin, TX 78712
Website: https://he.utexas.edu/txa
Contact: https://he.utexas.edu/about/contact
Request for Information: N/A
Phone: (512) 475-7399
Email: admissions@austin.utexas.edu

COST OF ATTENDANCE:

In-State Tuition & Fees: $10,824 | **Additional Expenses:** $16,904
Total: $27,728

Out-of-State Tuition & Fees: $38,326 | **Additional Expenses:** $16,904
Total: $55,230

Financial Aid: https://finaid.utexas.edu/

ADDITIONAL INFORMATION:

Available Degree(s)

- BS in Textile and Apparel, options:
  - Apparel, Function, and Technical Design
  - Textiles and Apparel Honors

Freshman Portfolio Requirement

There is no portfolio requirement.

Scholarships Offered

Students are automatically considered for institutional aid. However, students will not be considered for need-based aid if they do not submit a FAFSA. Students are encouraged to apply to private scholarships as well. For more information, visit: https://admissions.utexas.edu/afford/undergrad-scholarships

Special Opportunities

UT Austin hosts the Textiles and Apparel High School Challenge. In this competition, students must design an apparel or accessory using materials from the trash. Winners receive tickets to the TXA Fashion Show and a private backstage tour.

Students are encouraged to study abroad. Besides the general university study abroad options, students may participate in faculty-led programs specific to Textiles and Apparel. Recent trips have occurred during "Maymester" in France, India, and China. For more information, visit: https://he.utexas.edu/students/study-abroad

Students can study apparel, functional, and technical design, textile conservation, museum studies. Each includes hands-on experiences to understand intercultural customs, consumer behavior, apparel/fashion design, computer-aided design, fashion show production, garment conservation/museum management, and fiber and fabric testing. Students complete a capstone in high-profile venues and are offered opportunities to study bio-based fibers, specialized fabrics, and cutting-edge 3D technology.

UNIVERSITY OF THE INCARNATE WORD

Address: 4301 Broadway, San Antonio, TX 78209
Website: https://www.uiw.edu/smd/academics/undergraduate/
fashion-management/index.html Contact: https://www.uiw.edu/
contact/index.html
Request for Information: https://www.uiw.edu/gouiw/index.html
Phone: (210) 829-6005
Email: admis@uiwtx.edu

COST OF ATTENDANCE:

Tuition & Fees: $33,100 | **Additional Expenses:** $17,712
Total: $50,812

Financial Aid: https://www.uiw.edu/finaid/index.html

ADDITIONAL INFORMATION:

Available Degree(s)

- BS in Fashion Management, concentration: Apparel
  Production and Design

Freshman Portfolio Requirement

There is no portfolio requirement.

Scholarships Offered

The Jurren Sullivan Center for Fashion Management awards
fashion students scholarships that range from $500 to $1,500. For
more information, visit: https://www.uiw.edu/smd/academic-
programs/fashion/admissions/scholarships.html

Special Opportunities

Students may study abroad at UIW's sister school at the London
College of Fashion. For more information, visit: https://www.uiw.
edu/smd/academic-programs/fashion/study-abroad/index.html

ALABAMA

ARKANSAS

DELAWARE

DISTRICT OF
COLUMBIA

FLORIDA

GEORGIA

KENTUCKY

LOUISIANA

MARYLAND

MISSISSIPPI

NORTH CAROLINA

OKLAHOMA

SOUTH CAROLINA

TENNESSEE

TEXAS

VIRGINIA

WEST VIRGINIA

SOUTH

ALABAMA

ARKANSAS

DELAWARE

DISTRICT OF
COLUMBIA

FLORIDA

GEORGIA

KENTUCKY

LOUISIANA

MARYLAND

MISSISSIPPI

NORTH CAROLINA

OKLAHOMA

SOUTH CAROLINA

TENNESSEE

TEXAS

VIRGINIA

WEST VIRGINIA

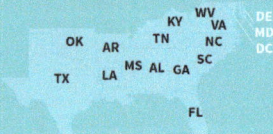

VIRGINIA COMMONWEALTH UNIVERSITY

Address: Virginia Commonwealth University, Richmond, VA 23284
Website: https://arts.vcu.edu/academics/departments/fashion/
Contact: https://www.vcu.edu/contacts/
Request for Information: https://www.vcu.edu/admissions/
contact-admissions/ugrad-interest-form/
Phone: (804) 828-0100
Email: ugrad@vcu.edu

COST OF ATTENDANCE:

In-State Tuition & Fees: $17,140 | **Additional Expenses:** $17,549
Total: $34,689

Out-of-State Tuition & Fees: $38,478 | **Additional Expenses:** $17,549
Total: $56,027

Financial Aid: https://finaid.vcu.edu/

ADDITIONAL INFORMATION:

Available Degree(s)

- BFA in Fashion, concentration: Fashion Design

Freshman Portfolio Requirement
- Submit via SlideRoom
- 12-16 strongest works of art created within the past two years
- Preference for diverse range of 2D and 3D media
- Recommend drawings from observation
- Discourage copying anime, cartoons, graffiti, or tattoos
- Videos optional (3 minutes max)

For more information, visit: https://arts.vcu.edu/admissions/how-
to-apply/freshman-applicants/freshman-applicants-visual-arts-
design/

Scholarships Offered
First-year students may be eligible for VCUarts talent scholarships
($5,000-$12,000 annually) if they apply by January 15th. Students
are automatically considered and eligibility is based on academic
merit and artistic talent. In addition, all students are automatically
considered for institutional scholarships if they apply by
November 15th. University scholarship awards vary based on the
scholarship, but range from $8,000 per year to $16,000 plus room
and board per year. For more information, visit: https://arts.vcu.
edu/admissions/scholarships/

Special Opportunities
VCUarts Qatar is the sister campus located in Doha, Qatar. Fashion
design and merchandising students may apply to spend a semester
at this campus. Additionally, students may study abroad over
the summer at the Santa Reparata International School of Art
in Florence, Italy. Fashion merchandising students may spend a
semester at the University of Westminster in London as well. For
more information, visit: https://arts.vcu.edu/study-abroad-fashion/

Notable Alumni
- Donwan Harrell: Fashion Designer and Founder of Prps and
  Akademiks

VIRGINIA POLYTECHNIC INSTITUTE AND STATE UNIVERSITY (VIRGINIA TECH)

Address: Virginia Polytechnic Institute and State University, Blacksburg, VA 24061
Website: https://liberalarts.vt.edu/academics/majors-and-minors/fashion-merchandising-and-design.html
Contact: https://vt.edu/contacts.html
Request for Information: https://vt.edu/admissions/forms/inquiry1.html
Phone: (540) 231-6267
Email: admissions@vt.edu

COST OF ATTENDANCE:

In-State Tuition & Fees: $14,175 | **Additional Expenses:** $9,876
Total: $24,051

Out-of-State Tuition & Fees: $33,857 | **Additional Expenses:** $9,876
Total: $43,733

Financial Aid: https://vt.edu/admissions/undergraduate/cost.html

ADDITIONAL INFORMATION:

Available Degree(s)

- BS in Fashion Merchandising and Design, specialization: Apparel Design and Production

Freshman Portfolio Requirement

There is no portfolio requirement.

Scholarships Offered

Students must submit a FAFSA for institutional and departmental scholarship/grant consideration. General scholarships range from $1,000-$3,000. Honors students may be eligible for additional scholarships. Additionally, the Presidential Campus Enrichment Grant is a renewable, competitive scholarship that is based on an essay question. For more information, visit: https://liberalarts.vt.edu/beyond-the-classroom/scholarships-and-awards.html

Special Opportunities

Students may participate in study tours or study abroad. The New York Fashion Study Tour is an opportunity for students to spend a week networking with fashion retailers and merchandisers. There are also guided tours of fashion houses. The European Study Abroad is offered every other summer and Involves visits with universities, design houses, and European boutiques in the following cities: London, Paris, Rome, Florence, and other fashion capitals. For more information, visit: https://liberalarts.vt.edu/departments-and-schools/apparel-housing-and-resource-management/why-study/study-abroad.html

ALABAMA

ARKANSAS

DELAWARE

DISTRICT OF COLUMBIA

FLORIDA

GEORGIA

KENTUCKY

LOUISIANA

MARYLAND

MISSISSIPPI

NORTH CAROLINA

OKLAHOMA

SOUTH CAROLINA

TENNESSEE

TEXAS

VIRGINIA

WEST VIRGINIA

SOUTH

CHAPTER 17

REGION FOUR

WEST

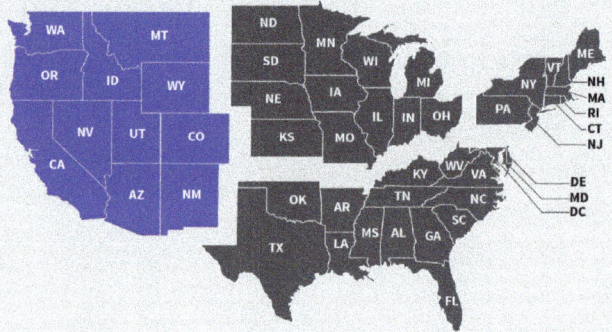

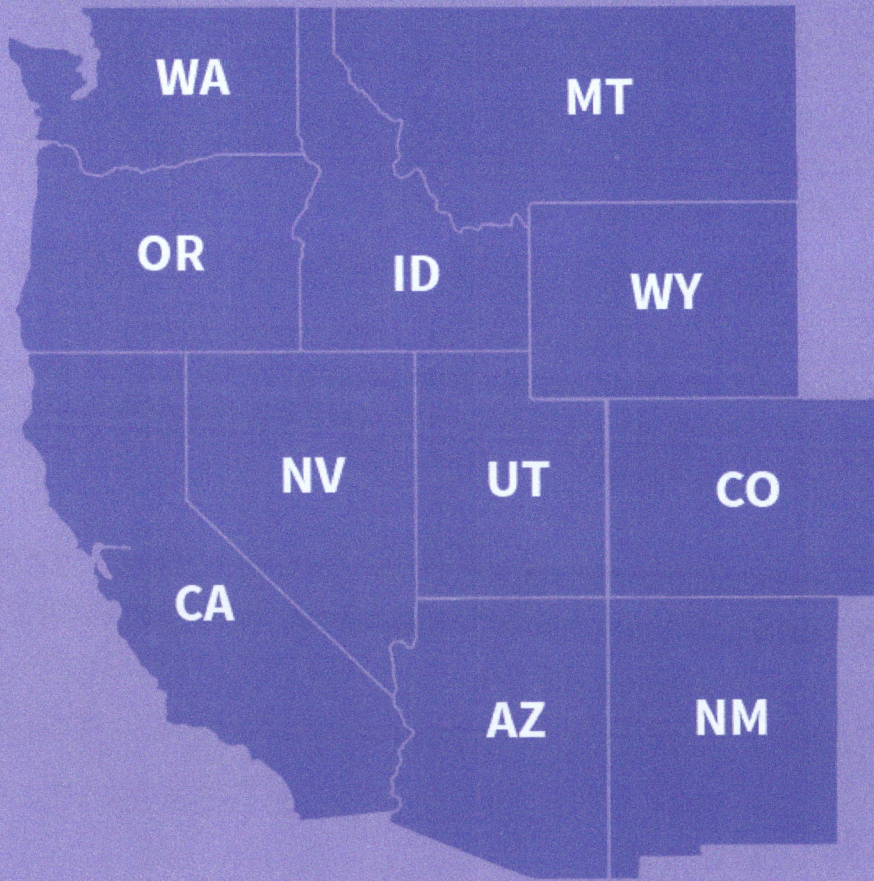

12 Programs | 13 States

1. CA - Academy of Art University
2. CA - California College of the Arts
3. CA - California State University, Long Beach (CSULB)
4. CA - California State University, Los Angeles (CSULA)
5. CA - California State University, Northridge (CSUN)
6. CA - Fashion Institute of Design and Merchandising (FIDM)
7. CA - Otis College of Art and Design
8. CA - San Francisco State University
9. CO - Colorado State University, Ft. Collins
10. HI - University of Hawaii at Manoa
11. OR - Oregon State University
12. WA - Washington State University

School	Avg. GPA, SAT Evidence-Based Reading Writing (ERW), SAT Math (M), and ACT Composite (C) Early Decision (ED): Yes/No	Admission Statistics	Program(s)	Portfolio and/or Interview Required (Req.)
Academy of Art University 79 New Montgomery St., San Francisco, CA 94105	GPA: N/A SAT (ERW): N/A SAT (M): N/A ACT (C): N/A *Academy of Art has an open admissions policy. ED: No	Admit Rate: N/A Undergrad Enrollment: 6,124 Total Enrollment: 8,928 Program Completion (2020): 77	BFA in Fashion Design BFA in Fashion Product Development BFA in Fashion Styling BFA in Footwear & Accessory Design BFA in Knitwear Design BFA in Textile Design	Portfolio: Not req. Interview: Not req.
California College of the Arts 1111 Eighth St., San Francisco, CA 94107	GPA: N/A SAT (ERW): N/A SAT (M): N/A ACT (C): N/A *California College of the Arts is test optional. ED: No	Admit Rate: 85% Undergrad Enrollment: 1,239 Total Enrollment: 1,612 Program Completion (2020): 20	BFA in Fashion Design BFA in Textiles	Portfolio: Req. Interview: Not req.

School	Avg. GPA, SAT Evidence-Based Reading Writing (ERW), SAT Math (M), and ACT Composite (C) Early Decision (ED): Yes/No	Admission Statistics	Program(s)	Portfolio and/or Interview Required (Req.)
California State University, Long Beach (CSULB) 1250 Bellflower Boulevard, Long Beach, CA 90840	GPA: 3.68 SAT (ERW): 510-620 SAT (M): 510-620 ACT (C): 20-26 ED: No	Admit Rate: 42% Undergrad Enrollment: 34,216 Total Enrollment: 40,069 Program Completion (2020): N/A	BA in Fashion Merchandising and Design, option: Fashion Design	Portfolio: Not req. Interview: Not req.
California State University, Los Angeles (CSULA) 5151 State University Dr, Los Angeles, CA 90032	GPA: 3.32 SAT (ERW): 440-530 SAT (M): 430-530 ACT (C): 15-20 ED: No	Admit Rate: 76% Undergrad Enrollment: 22,832 Total Enrollment: 26,745 Program Completion (2020): N/A	BA in Art, option: Fashion, Fiber, and Materials	Portfolio: Not req. Interview: Not req.
California State University, Northridge (CSUN) 18111 Nordhoff Street, Northridge, CA 91330	GPA: 3.39 SAT (ERW): 460-560 SAT (M): 440-550 ACT (C): 16-22 ED: No	Admit Rate: 66% Undergrad Enrollment: 34,916 Total Enrollment: 40,381 Program Completion (2020): N/A	BS in Apparel Design & Merchandising, concentrations: Apparel Design & Production Textile & Apparel	Portfolio: Not req. Interview: Not req.

WEST

FASHION DESIGN PROGRAMS

School	Avg. GPA, SAT Evidence-Based Reading Writing (ERW), SAT Math (M), and ACT Composite (C) Early Decision (ED): Yes/No	Admission Statistics	Program(s)	Portfolio and/or Interview Required (Req.)
Fashion Institute of Design and Merchandising (FIDM) 919 S. Grand Ave., Los Angeles, CA 90015	GPA: N/A SAT (ERW): N/A SAT (M): N/A ACT (C): N/A *FIDM is test optional. ED: No	Admit Rate: 39% Undergrad Enrollment: 1,847 Total Enrollment: 1,886 Program Completion (2020): N/A	BS in Apparel Technical Design BA in Fashion Knitwear Design	Portfolio: Req. Interview: Not req.
Otis College of Art and Design 9045 Lincoln Blvd., Los Angeles, CA 90045	GPA: N/A SAT (ERW): N/A SAT (M): N/A ACT (C): N/A *Otis College of Art and Design is test optional. ED: No	Admit Rate: 80% Undergrad Enrollment: 1,030 Total Enrollment: 1,073 Program Completion (2020): 21	BFA in Fashion Design	Portfolio: Req. Interview: Not req.
San Francisco State University 1600 Holloway Avenue - Burk Hall 329, San Francisco, CA 94132	GPA: 3.26 SAT (ERW): 470-580 SAT (M): 470-570 ACT (C): 17-23 ED: No	Admit Rate: 84% Undergrad Enrollment: 24,024 Total Enrollment: 27,349 Program Completion (2020): 41	BS in Apparel Design & Apparel Merchandising: concentration: Design	Portfolio: Not req. Interview: Not req.

School	Avg. GPA, SAT Evidence-Based Reading Writing (ERW), SAT Math (M), and ACT Composite (C) Early Decision (ED): Yes/No	Admission Statistics	Program(s)	Portfolio and/or Interview Required (Req.)
Colorado State University, Ft. Collins Colorado State University, Fort Collins, CO 80523	GPA: 3.7 SAT (ERW): 540-640 SAT (M): 530-640 ACT (C): 23-29 ED: No	Admit Rate: 84% Undergrad Enrollment: 24,792 Total Enrollment: 32,428 Program Completion (2020): 78	BS in Apparel and Merchandising, concentrations: Apparel Design and Production Product Development	Portfolio: Not req. Interview: Not req.
University of Hawaii at Manoa 2500 Campus Rd, Honolulu, HI 96822	GPA: 3.64 SAT (ERW): 540-630 SAT (M): 530-640 ACT (C): 21-26 ED: No	Admit Rate: 84% Undergrad Enrollment: 13,203 Total Enrollment: 18,025 Program Completion (2020): 21	BS in Fashion Design and Merchandising, specialization: Fashion Design	Portfolio: Not req. Interview: Not req.
Oregon State University Oregon State University, Corvallis, OR 97331	GPA: 3.62 SAT (ERW): 540-650 SAT (M): 540-660 ACT (C): 21-29 ED: No	Admit Rate: 82% Undergrad Enrollment: 26,644 Total Enrollment: 32,312 Program Completion (2020): 11	BS in Apparel Design	Portfolio: Not req. Interview: Not req.

WEST

FASHION DESIGN PROGRAMS

School	Avg. GPA, SAT Evidence-Based Reading Writing (ERW), SAT Math (M), and ACT Composite (C) Early Decision (ED): Yes/No	Admission Statistics	Program(s)	Portfolio and/or Interview Required (Req.)
Washington State University Washington State University, Pullman, WA 99164	GPA: 3.46 SAT (ERW): 510-610 SAT (M): 510-600 ACT (C): 20-26 ED: No	Admit Rate: 80% Undergrad Enrollment: 25,470 Total Enrollment: 31,159 Program Completion (2020): 58	BA in Apparel, Merchandising, Design, & Textile (AMDT), concentration: Apparel Design	Portfolio: Not req. Interview: Not req.

ALASKA

ARIZONA

CALIFORNIA

COLORADO

HAWAII

IDAHO

MONTANA

NEVADA

NEW MEXICO

OREGON

UTAH

WASHINGTON

WYOMING

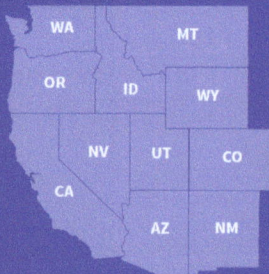

ACADEMY OF ART UNIVERSITY

Address: 79 New Montgomery St., San Francisco, CA 94105
Website: https://www.academyart.edu/academics/fashion/
Contact: https://my.academyart.edu/directories/admissions
Request for Information: https://www.academyart.edu/form-request-information/
Phone: (800) 544-2787
Email: admissions@academyart.edu

COST OF ATTENDANCE:

Tuition & Fees: $26,399 | **Additional Expenses:** N/A
Total: $26,399

Financial Aid: https://www.academyart.edu/finances/types-of-financial-aid/

ADDITIONAL INFORMATION:

Available Degree(s)

- BFA in Fashion Design
- BFA in Fashion Product Development
- BFA in Fashion Styling
- BFA in Footwear & Accessory Design
- BFA in Knitwear Design
- BFA in Textile Design

Freshman Portfolio Requirement

There is no portfolio requirement. This is an open-admissions school.

Scholarships Offered

The Emerging Artist Scholarship offers awards up to $3,000. Academy of Art also has information on nationwide scholarship opportunities with specific deadlines. Students are encouraged to regularly check on and apply to these scholarships. For more information, visit: https://www.academyart.edu/finances/scholarships/

Special Opportunities

The Academy houses a 3D Pattern Making Lab, a knitting studio, a pattern making studio, a styling closet, and a textile lab. The textile lab is fully equipped with 700 silkscreens, repeat yardage tables, UV exposure units, and pigments and dyes. For more information, visit: https://www.academyart.edu/academics/fashion/facilities/

A graduation portfolio review is held every Spring. All graduating students can showcase their portfolios to guests and industry professionals. To see previous shows, visit: https://www.academyart.edu/academics/fashion/fashion-shows/

Notable Alumni

- Lauren Conrad: Author, Fashion Designer, and Actress on reality television series *The Hills* and *Laguna Beach: The Real Orange County.*
- Heidi Montag: Fashion Designer, Singer, and Actress on reality television series *The Hills*
- Kara Laricks: Fashion Designer and season one winner of the show *Fashion Star.*

CALIFORNIA COLLEGE OF THE ARTS

Address: 1111 Eighth St., San Francisco, CA 94107
Website: https://www.cca.edu/design/fashion-design/
Contact: Contact via phone or email.
Request for Information: https://www.cca.edu/admissions/info/
Phone: (800) 447-1278
Email: info@cca.edu

COST OF ATTENDANCE:

Tuition & Fees: $52,312 | **Additional Expenses:** $24,067
Total: $76,871

Financial Aid: https://www.cca.edu/admissions/tuition/#section-financial-aid

ADDITIONAL INFORMATION:

Available Degree(s)

- BFA in Fashion Design
- BFA in Textiles

Freshman Portfolio Requirement

- Submit via SlideRoom
- 10-15 of your best work
- Stand-alone film/animation samples should not exceed five minutes

For more information, visit: https://www.cca.edu/admissions/undergraduate/#section-how-to-apply

Scholarships Offered

Merit-based, need-based, CCA-named, and other scholarships available. For more information, visit: https://www.cca.edu/admissions/financial-aid/#section-scholarships

Special Opportunities

CCA houses the Soft Lab. This lab has an electronic embroidery machine. In this lab, students create fabric, textile, and woven projects. Students attend an orientation to learn more about how to use these facilities. For more information, visit: https://portal.cca.edu/learning/shops/soft-lab/

Notable Alumni

- Liam Cliff, Zewei Hong, Jennifer Wang selected for CFDA Fashion Future Showcase
- Kay Sekimachi: Fiber Artist known for her 3D woven monofilament hangings

ALASKA

ARIZONA

CALIFORNIA

COLORADO

HAWAII

IDAHO

MONTANA

NEVADA

NEW MEXICO

OREGON

UTAH

WASHINGTON

WYOMING

WEST

ALASKA

ARIZONA

CALIFORNIA

COLORADO

HAWAII

IDAHO

MONTANA

NEVADA

NEW MEXICO

OREGON

UTAH

WASHINGTON

WYOMING

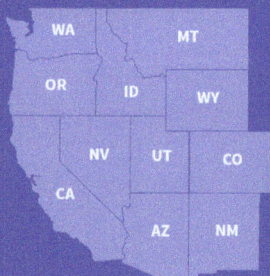

CALIFORNIA STATE UNIVERSITY, LONG BEACH (CSULB)

Address: 1250 Bellflower Boulevard, Long Beach, CA 90840
Website: https://www.csulb.edu/college-of-health-human-services/family-and-consumer-sciences/fashion-design
Contact: https://www.csulb.edu/contact
Request for Information: https://web.csulb.edu/divisions/students/uosr/request_info.html
Phone: (562) 985-4111
Email: eslb@csulb.edu

COST OF ATTENDANCE:

In-State Tuition & Fees: $6,846 | **Additional Expenses:** $18,206
Total: $25,386

Out-of-State Tuition & Fees: $17,142 | **Additional Expenses:** $18,540
Total: $35,682

Financial Aid: https://www.csulb.edu/student-affairs/financial-aid-and-scholarships-office

ADDITIONAL INFORMATION:

Available Degree(s)

- BA in Fashion Merchandising and Design, option: Fashion Design

Freshman Portfolio Requirement

There is no portfolio requirement.

Scholarships Offered

The President's Scholars Program offers merit-based scholarships to students admitted to the University Honors Program (UHP). Benefits not only include a financial award, but also priority registration, individualized academic advising, smaller classes, and "the opportunity to participate in Honors House, the on-campus residential honors community". Students may apply for BeachScholarships once they are admitted into CSULB. For more information, visit: https://www.csulb.edu/student-affairs/financial-aid-and-scholarships-office/prospective-students

Special Opportunities

Fashion students may participate in a fashion study tour where they visit museums, apparel manufacturers, retailers, and apparel design businesses. Tours are conducted throughout the year in locations such as New York City, Paris, and Italy.

Notable Alumni

- Amber Corwin: skating costume designer, former figure skater
- Cathy Cooper: Wardrobe Stylist/Costume Designer for the Los Angeles Philharmonic and commercials for Nike, Heineken, and Ford
- Phillip Lim: 3.1 Phillip Lim, won Council of Fashion Designers of America, Accessory Designer of the Year Award Swarovski Menswear & Womenswear Award

CALIFORNIA STATE UNIVERSITY, LOS ANGELES (CSULA)

Address: 5151 State University Dr, Los Angeles, CA 90032
Website: http://www.calstatela.edu/academic/art/fashion.php
Contact: https://www.calstatela.edu/contact-us
Request for Information: N/A
Phone: (323) 343-3000
Email: admission@calstatela.edu

COST OF ATTENDANCE:

In-State Tuition & Fees: $6,782 | **Additional Expenses:** $21,219
Total: $28,001

Out-of-State Tuition & Fees: $16,286 | **Additional Expenses:** $21,219
Total: $37,505

Financial Aid: https://www.calstatela.edu/financialaid

ADDITIONAL INFORMATION:

Available Degree(s)

- BA in Art, option: Fashion, Fiber, and Materials

Freshman Portfolio Requirement

There is no portfolio requirement.

Scholarships Offered

The CSU Trustee's Awards for Outstanding Achievement is need-based and merit-based. The award ranges from $1,000-$15,000 and is open to any major. Students must apply and be currently enrolled full-time. Students are also encouraged to apply to outside scholarships. For more information, visit: https://www.calstatela.edu/financialaid/scholarships

Special Opportunities

Students may obtain an undergraduate certificate in Fashion Retailing or Fashion, Fiber and Materials.

ALASKA

ARIZONA

CALIFORNIA

COLORADO

HAWAII

IDAHO

MONTANA

NEVADA

NEW MEXICO

OREGON

UTAH

WASHINGTON

WYOMING

WEST

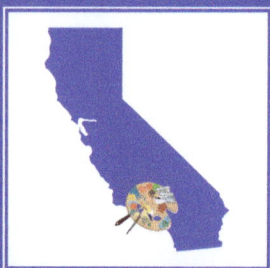

ALASKA

ARIZONA

CALIFORNIA

COLORADO

HAWAII

IDAHO

MONTANA

NEVADA

NEW MEXICO

OREGON

UTAH

WASHINGTON

WYOMING

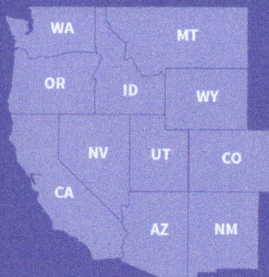

CALIFORNIA STATE UNIVERSITY, NORTHRIDGE

Address: 18111 Nordhoff Street, Northridge, CA 91330
Website: https://www.csun.edu/health-human-development/family-consumer-sciences/program-overview-0
Contact: https://www.csun.edu/contact
Request for Information: N/A
Phone: (818) 677-1200
Email: outreach.recruitment.@csun.edu

COST OF ATTENDANCE:

In-State Tuition & Fees: $6,972 | **Additional Expenses:** $16,670
Total: $23,642

Out-of-State Tuition & Fees: $16,476 | **Additional Expenses:** $16,670
Total: $33,146

Financial Aid: https://www.csun.edu/financialaid/financial-aid-basics

ADDITIONAL INFORMATION:

Available Degree(s)

- BS in Apparel Design & Merchandising, concentrations:
  o Apparel Design & Production
  o Textile & Apparel

Freshman Portfolio Requirement

There is no portfolio requirement.

Scholarships Offered

CSUN offers several different scholarships to incoming students. It is suggested that students look through current scholarship opportunities, as they are constantly changing. For more information, visit: https://csun.academicworks.com/

California residents may be eligible for CSU Grants. For more information, visit: https://www.csun.edu/financialaid/california-state-university-grants

Special Opportunities

CSUN houses a collection of historical garments that are displayed in galleries on campus as a visual aid for students during lectures.

FASHION INSTITUTE OF DESIGN AND MERCHANDISING (FIDM)

Address: 919 S. Grand Ave., Los Angeles, CA 90015
Website: https://fidm.edu/
Contact: https://fidm.edu/en/about/contact+us/
Request for Information: https://go.fidm.edu/info
Phone: (800) 624-1200
Email: admissions@fidm.edu
Other locations: San Francisco, CA; Irvine, CA; San Diego, CA

COST OF ATTENDANCE:

Tuition & Fees: $31,465 | **Additional Expenses:** $22,373
Total: $53,838

Financial Aid: https://fidm.edu/en/admissions/financial+aid/

ADDITIONAL INFORMATION:

Available Degree(s)

- BS in Apparel Technical Design
- BA in Fashion Knitwear Design

Freshman Portfolio Requirement

To enter the BS in Apparel Technical Design or any baccalaureate program, applicants must complete an AA degree first. AA degrees related to fashion to consider include: Apparel Industry Management; Footwear Design & Development; Fashion Design; and Textile Design.

Note: AA Advanced Study degrees are also offered. However, these degrees are for students who already hold a degree.

- Submit via Application Portal
- 8-12 examples of your work
- May focus on one medium or show a variety of media

For more information, visit: https://fidm.edu/en/admissions/how+to+apply/

Scholarships Offered

The FFCLA National Scholarship Competition offers a full year of tuition to first place winners. In addition, high school juniors who are active members of the official FIDM Fashion Club are eligible to enter the FIDM Fashion Club Junior Scholarship Competition. High school seniors may be eligible for the FIDM National Scholarship Competition (covering one year of tuition). Additionally, the GUESS Scholars Program is available to high school seniors, high school graduates, college transfers, or continuing FIDM students. This program offers a full, one-year scholarship for tuition and supplies. For more information, visit: https://fidm.edu/en/admissions/financial+aid/scholarships/

Special Opportunities

Students are encouraged to embark on one of the Study Tours – domestic and international opportunities for students. Study tours consist of an expert guiding the tour and many of these experiences include a networking element. Study tours take place in France, Italy, and China. For more information, visit: https://fidm.edu/en/student+life/study+abroad/study+tours/

187

ALASKA

ARIZONA

CALIFORNIA

COLORADO

HAWAII

IDAHO

MONTANA

NEVADA

NEW MEXICO

OREGON

UTAH

WASHINGTON

WYOMING

WEST

ALASKA

ARIZONA

CALIFORNIA

COLORADO

HAWAII

IDAHO

MONTANA

NEVADA

NEW MEXICO

OREGON

UTAH

WASHINGTON

WYOMING

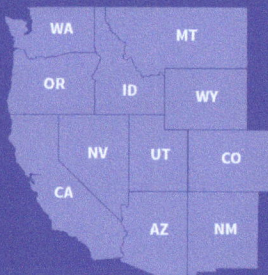

OTIS COLLEGE OF ART AND DESIGN

Address: 9045 Lincoln Blvd., Los Angeles, CA 90045
Website: https://www.otis.edu/fashion-design
Contact: https://www.otis.edu/contact-otis-college-art-design
Request for Information: https://www.otis.edu/inquiry-form
Phone: (310) 665-6800
Email: admissions@otis.edu

COST OF ATTENDANCE:

Tuition & Fees: $47,700 | **Additional Expenses:** $20,175
Total: $67,875

Financial Aid: https://www.otis.edu/financial-aid

ADDITIONAL INFORMATION:

Available Degree(s)

- BFA in Fashion Design

Freshman Portfolio Requirement

- Submit via SlideRoom
- Submit an Open Portfolio or a Structured Portfolio
- Open Portfolio
  - o 10-20 examples of best and most recent work
  - o Artwork can be in any medium
  - o Applicants who have work that is digital or photo/ video based should include 5 examples of work in other mediums
  - o Encouraged to include direct observation
- Structured Portfolio
  - o 3 images that function as portraits, without showing a face
  - o 4 images to tell a story
  - o 3 images to showcase places that are important to you

For more information, visit: https://www.otis.edu/portfolio

Scholarships Offered

Otis College Scholarships are awarded to students based on need, academic merit, and artistic merit. Otis Named Scholarships are awarded by donors such as Nike or Sony for students who maintain a 3.0+ GPA and typically requires a recommendation from your department chair. Otis College also recommends students apply for outside scholarships. For more information, visit: https://www.otis.edu/financial-aid/scholarships

Special Opportunities

Junior-level and Senior-level students present their work at the annual Scholarship Benefit and Fashion Show. In addition, they showcase their work in the Neiman Marcus windows in Beverly Hills. For information on the Scholarship Benefit and Fashion Show, visit: https://www.otis.edu/fashion-design/fashion-show

For information on the Neiman Marcus Window Display, visit: https://www.otis.edu/fashion-design/neiman-marcus-window-display

Notable Alumni

- Dahn Tran: Won "Shark Tank"

SAN FRANCISCO STATE UNIVERSITY

Address: 1600 Holloway Avenue - Burk Hall 329, San Francisco, CA 94132
Website: https://fina.sfsu.edu/adm
Contact: https://fina.sfsu.edu/contactus
Request for Information: N/A
Phone: (415) 338-1219
Email: fina@sfsu.edu

COST OF ATTENDANCE:

In-State Tuition & Fees: $7,270 | **Additional Expenses:** $18,858
Total: $26,128

Out-of-State Tuition & Fees: $16,774 | **Additional Expenses:** $18,858
Total: $35,632

Financial Aid: https://financialaid.sfsu.edu/

ADDITIONAL INFORMATION:

Available Degree(s)

- BS in Apparel Design & Apparel Merchandising: concentration: Design

Freshman Portfolio Requirement

There is no portfolio requirement.

Scholarships Offered

The Department of Family, Interiors, Nutrition, and Apparel (FINA) offers scholarships specific to FINA students. Students are encouraged to visit the link for more information, since scholarship availability changes throughout the course of the year. For more information, visit: https://fina.sfsu.edu/content/student-resources#Scholarships

Special Opportunities

Students are encouraged to study abroad. For more information, visit: https://oip.sfsu.edu/sfstateabroad

ALASKA

ARIZONA

CALIFORNIA

COLORADO

HAWAII

IDAHO

MONTANA

NEVADA

NEW MEXICO

OREGON

UTAH

WASHINGTON

WYOMING

WEST

ALASKA

ARIZONA

CALIFORNIA

COLORADO

HAWAII

IDAHO

MONTANA

NEVADA

NEW MEXICO

OREGON

UTAH

WASHINGTON

WYOMING

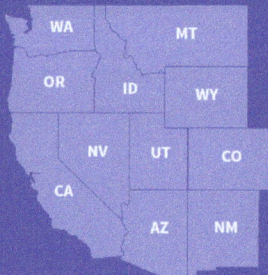

COLORADO STATE UNIVERSITY, FT. COLLINS

Address: Colorado State University, Fort Collins, CO 80523
Website: https://www.chhs.colostate.edu/dm/
Contact: https://admissions.colostate.edu/contactus/
Request for Information: https://www.chhs.colostate.edu/
academics/request-info/
Phone: (970) 491-6331
Email: chhsinfo@colostate.edu

COST OF ATTENDANCE:

In-State Tuition & Fees: $12,432 | **Additional Expenses:** $17,163
Total: $29,595

Out-of-State Tuition & Fees: $31,712 | **Additional Expenses:** $17,862
Total: $49,574

Financial Aid: https://financialaid.colostate.edu/

ADDITIONAL INFORMATION:

Available Degree(s)

- BS in Apparel and Merchandising, concentrations:
  o Apparel Design and Production
  o Product Development

Freshman Portfolio Requirement
There is no portfolio requirement.

Scholarships Offered
The College of Health and Human Sciences offers a few scholarship opportunities to students within this department. Fashion students may be eligible for the Students First Scholarship, which awards students who are active in community service organizations and have a 3.0+ GPA. For more information on available College of Health and Human Sciences scholarships, visit: https://www.chhs.colostate.edu/academics/scholarships/

Colorado State University at Ft. Collins offers institutional aid for students of any major. Out-of-state students may be eligible for the Presidential, Provost's, Dean's, or Academic Recognition Scholarships ($20,000-$40,000). In-state students are also eligible for merit scholarships, with awards ranging from $4,000 to $16,000. For more information, visit: https://financialaid.colostate.edu/scholarships/

Special Opportunities
Every other year, the Department offers a study tour of New York City to students. This week-long trip has "students [visiting] firms in the apparel and interior design industries and engage in a variety of cultural and entertainment activities, which may include visiting historic sites and museums, taking in a Manhattan dinner cruise, and attending Broadway shows."

International study tours are also available and highly relevant to Apparel & Merchandising students. Previous destinations have been in Hong Kong, Thailand, and England/Scotland. For more information, visit: https://www.chhs.colostate.edu/dm/programs-and-degrees/advising-and-support/study-tours-and-education-abroad/

Students may also opt for a traditional study abroad experience through Colorado State.

UNIVERSITY OF HAWAII AT MANOA

Address: 2500 Campus Rd, Honolulu, HI 96822
Website: https://cms.ctahr.hawaii.edu/Majors/FDM
Contact: https://manoa.hawaii.edu/about/contact/
Request for Information: https://manoa.hawaii.edu/admissions/request/
Phone: (800) 823-9771
Email: uhmanoa.admissions@hawaii.edu

COST OF ATTENDANCE:

In-State Tuition & Fees: $12,186 | **Additional Expenses:** $17,734
Total: $29,920

WUE* Tuition & Fees: $17,838 | **Additional Expenses:** $17,734
Total: $35,572

Out-of-State Tuition & Fees: $34,218 | **Additional Expenses:** $17,734
Total: $51,952

*Western Undergraduate Exchange (WUE) is a special tuition program for students from certain states. For a list of eligible states, visit: https://manoa.hawaii.edu/admissions/financing/wue.html

Financial Aid: https://manoa.hawaii.edu/admissions/financing/index.html

ADDITIONAL INFORMATION:

Available Degree(s)

- BS in Fashion Design and Merchandising, specialization: Fashion Design

Freshman Portfolio Requirement

There is no portfolio requirement.

Scholarships Offered

The College of Tropical Agriculture and Human Resources (CTAHR) offers incoming fashion students scholarship opportunities that range from $2,000 upwards. For more information, visit: https://cms.ctahr.hawaii.edu/Students/Scholarships

There are also a few scholarships for fashion students while they are undergraduates. For more information, visit: https://cms.ctahr.hawaii.edu/fcs/Undergraduate/FDM/Scholarships

Additionally, incoming in-state, out-of-state, and international students may be eligible for merit-based scholarships. For more information, visit: http://www.hawaii.edu/fas/info/automatic_admissions_scholarships.php

Special Opportunities

UHM hosts an annual fashion show where apparel design students showcase their work. For more information, visit: https://cms.ctahr.hawaii.edu/fcs2/Undergraduate/FDM/UHM-Fashion-Shows

ALASKA

ARIZONA

CALIFORNIA

COLORADO

HAWAII

IDAHO

MONTANA

NEVADA

NEW MEXICO

OREGON

UTAH

WASHINGTON

WYOMING

WEST

ALASKA

ARIZONA

CALIFORNIA

COLORADO

HAWAII

IDAHO

MONTANA

NEVADA

NEW MEXICO

OREGON

UTAH

WASHINGTON

WYOMING

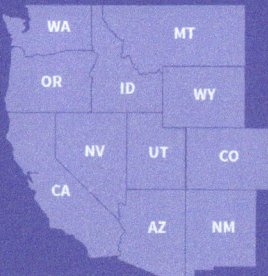

OREGON STATE UNIVERSITY

Address: Oregon State University, Corvallis, OR 97331
Website: http://business.oregonstate.edu/programs/undergraduate/apparel-design
Contact: https://admissions.oregonstate.edu/contact-information
Request for Information: https://admissions.oregonstate.edu/send-me-info
Phone: (541) 737-4411
Email: osuadmit@oregonstate.edu

COST OF ATTENDANCE:

In-State Tuition & Fees: $12,165 | **Additional Expenses:** $17,142
Total: $29,307

Out-of-State Tuition & Fees: $32,355 | **Additional Expenses:** $17,142
Total: $49,497

Financial Aid: https://financialaid.oregonstate.edu/

ADDITIONAL INFORMATION:

Available Degree(s)

- BS in Apparel Design

Freshman Portfolio Requirement

There is no portfolio requirement for first-year applicants. Students enter as a pre-Apparel Design major and undergo a competitive review for entry into the major.

Scholarships Offered

Oregon State offers institutional aid to students of any major. Out-of-state applicants may be eligible for the Provost Scholarship, or specific scholarships only available to CA, WA, HI, or ID residents. Oregon State residents may be eligible for the merit-based Presidential Scholarship (up to $10,000 per year for four years), or a number of other scholarships. For more information, visit: https://scholarships.oregonstate.edu/prospective-student-scholarships

Special Opportunities

Students may study abroad at the Accademia Italiana in Florence, Italy, the London College of Fashion, or Hanyang University in Seoul. For more information, visit: http://business.oregonstate.edu/student-experience/student-success/study-abroad

Notable Alumni

- Almarina Bianchi: Former Product Integrity Manager, Pendleton Woolen Mills, Advisory Board at T.A.N.G. Apparel and Footwear, Sr. Product Manager, Nike
- Jamie (Cheung) Holzkamp: Product Developer, Columbia Sportswear
- Teresa Durbin: Merchandise Manager, Nike

WASHINGTON STATE UNIVERSITY

Address: Washington State University, Pullman, WA 99164
Website: http://amdt.wsu.edu/major/
Contact: https://admission.wsu.edu/contact/
Request for Information: https://admission.wsu.edu/contact/request-info/
Phone: (888) 468-6978
Email: admissions@wsu.edu

COST OF ATTENDANCE:

In-State Tuition & Fees: $12,416 | **Additional Expenses:** $12,082
Total: $24,498

Out-of-State Tuition & Fees: $27,732 | **Additional Expenses:** $12,082
Total: $39,814

Financial Aid: https://admission.wsu.edu/tuition-costs/tuition-break-down/

ADDITIONAL INFORMATION:

Available Degree(s)

- BA in Apparel, Merchandising, Design, & Textile (AMDT), concentration: Apparel Design

Freshman Portfolio Requirement

There is no portfolio requirement.

Scholarships Offered

The College of Agricultural, Human, and Natural Resource Sciences offer departmental scholarships the range in value from $100 to $4,000. Apparel, Merchandising, Design, & Textile (AMDT) students are eligible for these. Students can gain access to these awards by applying to the WSU online scholarship application. For more information, visit: https://cahnrs.wsu.edu/academics/scholarships/?

There are many scholarships specific to Washington residents, out-of-state students, and international students. In-state scholarships are merit and/or need-based and go up to full tuition. Out-of-state scholarships go up to $11,000 per year, for four years. International scholarships range from $1,000-$2,000 per semester. For more information, visit: https://admission.wsu.edu/scholarships/

Special Opportunities

Given the global nature of the fashion world, AMDT students are especially encouraged to study abroad. WSU suggests that students plan early in their college career due to sequencing of courses. In addition, summers abroad are the most preferable choice for AMDT majors.

ALASKA

ARIZONA

CALIFORNIA

COLORADO

HAWAII

IDAHO

MONTANA

NEVADA

NEW MEXICO

OREGON

UTAH

WASHINGTON

WYOMING

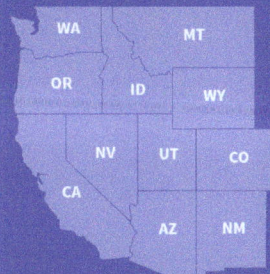

WEST

CHAPTER 18

FASHION DESIGN SCHOOLS BY CITY/ STATE

School	City	State
Auburn University	Auburn	Alabama
California State University, Long Beach (CSULB)	Long Beach	California
California State University, Los Angeles (CSULA)	Los Angeles	California
Fashion Institute of Design and Merchandising (FIDM)	Los Angeles	California
Otis College of Art and Design	Los Angeles	California
California State University, Northridge (CSUN)	Northridge	California
Academy of Art University	San Francisco	California
California College of the Arts	San Francisco	California
San Francisco State University	San Francisco	California
Colorado State University, Ft. Collins	Fort Collins	Colorado
Delaware State University	Dover	Delaware
University of Delaware	Newark	Delaware
Miami International University Art & Design	Miami	Florida
Savannah College of Art & Design (SCAD)	Savannah	Georgia
University of Hawaii at Manoa	Honolulu	Hawaii
Columbia College Chicago	Chicago	Illinois
School of the Art Institute of Chicago (SAIC)	Chicago	Illinois
Dominican University	River Forest	Illinois
Indiana University Bloomington	Bloomington	Indiana
Iowa State University	Ames	Iowa
Kansas State University	Manhattan	Kansas
Louisiana State University	Baton Rouge	Louisiana
Maryland Institute College of Art (MICA)	Baltimore	Maryland
Massachusetts College of Art & Design (MassArt)	Boston	Massachusetts
Michigan State University	East Lansing	Michigan
University of Minnesota	Minneapolis	Minnesota
Stephens College	Columbia	Missouri
Washington University in St. Louis	St. Louis	Missouri
University of Nebraska	Lincoln	Nebraska
Pratt Institute	Brooklyn	New York
Cornell University	Ithaca	New York
Fashion Inst. of Tech (FIT)	New York	New York
Parsons - The New School	New York	New York

School	City	State
Marist College	Poughkeepsie	New York
Syracuse University	Syracuse	New York
University of North Carolina at Greensboro	Greensboro	North Carolina
North Carolina State, Raleigh College of Design	Raleigh	North Carolina
University of Cincinnati	Cincinnati	Ohio
Columbus College of Art & Design	Columbus	Ohio
Kent State University	Kent	Ohio
Oklahoma State University	Stillwater	Oklahoma
Oregon State University	Corvallis	Oregon
Drexel University	Philadelphia	Pennsylvania
Moore College of Art & Design	Philadelphia	Pennsylvania
Thomas Jefferson University	Philadelphia	Pennsylvania
Rhode Island School of Design (RISD)	Providence	Rhode Island
University of Rhode Island	South Kingston	Rhode Island
University of Texas, Austin	Austin	Texas
Texas Woman's University	Denton	Texas
University of North Texas	Denton	Texas
Texas Tech University	Lubbock	Texas
University of the Incarnate Word	San Antonio	Texas
Baylor University	Waco	Texas
Virginia Polytechnic Institute and State University (Virginia Tech)	Blacksburg	Virginia
Virginia Commonwealth University	Richmond	Virginia
Washington State University	Pullman	Washington

CHAPTER 19

TOP 25 FASHION DESIGN PROGRAMS

Ranking	School
1	Fashion Institute of Technology, NY
2	Savannah College of Art & Design, GA
3	Parsons School of Design, NY
4	Fashion Institute of Design & Merchandising, CA
5	Pratt Institute, NY
6	Drexel University, PA
7	Rhode Island School of Design, RI
8	Kent State University, OH
9	Cornell University, NY
10	Academy of Art University, CA
11	Iowa State University, IA
12	Marist College, NY
13	North Carolina State University, NC
14	Colorado State University, CO
15	Otis College of Art & Design, CA
16	Auburn University, AL
17	University of Minnesota, MN
18	Thomas Jefferson University, PA
19	University of Delaware, DE
20	University of Texas, Austin, TX
21	Baylor University, TX
22	School of the Art Institute of Chicago, IL
23	LIM College, NY
24	University of North Texas, TX
25	University of North Carolina at Greensboro, NC

Source: https://www.fashion-schools.org/articles/top-50-fashion-design-schools-and-colleges-us-2021-rankings

CHAPTER 20

FASHION DESIGN SCHOOLS BY AVERAGE TEST SCORE

FASHION DESIGN SCHOOLS BY AVERAGE SAT SCORE

School	Avg. SAT
Delaware State University	420-520 (ERW)
	390-490 (M)
California State University, Los Angeles (CSULA)	440-530 (ERW)
	430-530 (M)
California State University, Northridge (CSUN)	460-570 (ERW)
	450-560 (M)
San Francisco State University	470-570 (ERW)
	460-560 (M)
Texas Woman's University	480-580 (ERW)
	460-560 (M)
University of the Incarnate Word	480-580 (ERW)
	470-560 (M)
Dominican University	480-580 (ERW)
	480-580 (M)
Iowa State University	480-630 (ERW)
	530-680 (M)
University of North Carolina at Greensboro	490-590 (ERW)
	490-570 (M)
Kent State University	510-610 (ERW)
	510-600 (M)
Washington State University	510-610 (ERW)
	510-600 (M)
California State University, Long Beach (CSULB)	510-620 (ERW)
	510-620 (M)
Oklahoma State University	510-630 (ERW)
	510-620 (M)
University of North Texas	530-630 (ERW)
	520-610 (M)
Texas Tech University	540-620 (ERW)
	530-620 (M)
University of Hawaii at Manoa	540-630 (ERW)
	530-640 (M)
Savannah College of Art & Design (SCAD)	540-640 (ERW)
	500-600 (M)

School	Avg. SAT
Virginia Commonwealth University	540-640 (ERW)
	520-610 (M)
Colorado State University, Ft. Collins	540-640 (ERW)
	530-640 (M)
Oregon State University	540-650 (ERW)
	540-660 (M)
University of Rhode Island	550-630 (ERW)
	540-630 (M)
Thomas Jefferson University	550-630 (ERW)
	540-640 (M)
Michigan State University	550-640 (ERW)
	550-660 (M)
University of Nebraska	550-650 (ERW)
	560-670 (M)
Louisiana State University	550-660 (ERW)
	540-640 (M)
University of Cincinnati	560-650 (ERW)
	560-680 (M)
School of the Art Institute of Chicago (SAIC)	560-660 (ERW)
	480-600 (M)
Indiana University Bloomington	560-670 (ERW)
	560-680 (M)
Pratt Institute	570-660 (ERW)
	550-680 (M)
Marist College	580-660 (ERW)
	560-660 (M)
University of Delaware	580-660 (ERW)
	570-670 (M)
Syracuse University	580-670 (ERW)
	600-710 (M)
Parsons - The New School	580-680 (ERW)
	560-680 (M)
Auburn University	590-650 (ERW)
	580-680 (M)
Virginia Polytechnic Institute and State University (Virginia Tech)	590-680 (ERW)
	580-690 (M)

School	Avg. SAT
Drexel University	590-680 (ERW) 590-700 (M)
Baylor University	600-680 (ERW) 590-680 (M)
Stephens College	600-700 (ERW) 640-760 (M)
University of Minnesota	600-700 (ERW) 640-760 (M)
North Carolina State, Raleigh College of Design	610-690 (ERW) 620-720 (M)
Rhode Island School of Design (RISD)	610-700 (ERW) 640-770 (M)
University of Texas, Austin	610-720 (ERW) 600-750 (M)
Cornell University	680-750 (ERW) 720-790 (M)
Washington University in St. Louis	720-760 (ERW) 760-800 (M)
Kansas State University	N/A
Massachusetts College of Art & Design (MassArt)	N/A *Not req.
Columbia College Chicago	N/A *Test optional
Columbus College of Art & Design	N/A *Test optional
Fashion Inst. of Tech (FIT)	N/A *Test optional
Moore College of Art & Design	N/A *Test optional
Academy of Art University	N/A *Open admissions
Miami International University Art & Design	N/A *Open admissions
California College of the Arts	N/A *Test optional
Fashion Institute of Design and Merchandising (FIDM)	N/A *Test optional
Maryland Institute College of Art (MICA)	N/A *Test optional
Otis College of Art and Design	N/A *Test optional

FASHION DESIGN SCHOOLS BY AVERAGE ACT SCORE

School	Avg. ACT
California State University, Los Angeles (CSULA)	15-20 (ACT C)
California State University, Northridge (CSUN)	16-22 (ACT C)
Texas Woman's University	16-22 (ACT C)
San Francisco State University	16-23 (ACT C)
Delaware State University	17-22 (ACT C)
University of the Incarnate Word	17-23 (ACT C)
Dominican University	19-24 (ACT C)
University of North Carolina at Greensboro	19-25 (ACT C)
California State University, Long Beach (CSULB)	20-26 (ACT C)
Kent State University	20-26 (ACT C)
Washington State University	20-26 (ACT C)
Kansas State University	20-27 (ACT C)
Savannah College of Art & Design (SCAD)	20-27 (ACT C)
Thomas Jefferson University	20-27 (ACT C)
University of North Texas	20-27 (ACT C)
University of Hawaii at Manoa	21-26 (ACT C)
Iowa State University	21-28 (ACT C)
Oklahoma State University	21-28 (ACT C)
Virginia Commonwealth University	21-28 (ACT C)
Oregon State University	21-29 (ACT C)
School of the Art Institute of Chicago (SAIC)	22-25 (ACT C)
Texas Tech University	22-27 (ACT C)
University of Nebraska	22-28 (ACT C)
Louisiana State University	23-28 (ACT C)
University of Rhode Island	23-28 (ACT C)
Colorado State University, Ft. Collins	23-29 (ACT C)
Michigan State University	23-29 (ACT C)
University of Cincinnati	23-29 (ACT C)
Auburn University	24-30 (ACT C)
Indiana University Bloomington	24-31 (ACT C)
Pratt Institute	25-30 (ACT C)
University of Delaware	25-30 (ACT C)
Drexel University	25-31 (ACT C)
Stephens College	25-31 (ACT C)
University of Minnesota	25-31 (ACT C)

School	Avg. ACT
Virginia Polytechnic Institute and State University (Virginia Tech)	25-31 (ACT C)
Parsons - The New School	26-30 (ACT C)
Syracuse University	26-30 (ACT C)
Baylor University	26-31 (ACT C)
Marist College	26-31 (ACT C)
University of Texas, Austin	26-33 (ACT C)
North Carolina State, Raleigh College of Design	27-32 (ACT C)
Rhode Island School of Design (RISD)	27-32 (ACT C)
Cornell University	32-35 (ACT C)
Washington University in St. Louis	33-35 (ACT C)
Massachusetts College of Art & Design (MassArt)	N/A *Not req.
Academy of Art University	N/A *Open admissions
Miami International University Art & Design	N/A *Open admissions
Columbia College Chicago	N/A *Test optional
Columbus College of Art & Design	N/A *Test optional
Fashion Inst. of Tech (FIT)	N/A *Test optional
Moore College of Art & Design	N/A *Test optional
California College of the Arts	N/A *Test optional
Fashion Institute of Design and Merchandising (FIDM)	N/A *Test optional
Maryland Institute College of Art (MICA)	N/A *Test optional
Otis College of Art and Design	N/A *Test optional

FASHION DESIGN SCHOOLS BY AVERAGE GPA

School	Avg. GPA
Texas Woman's University	3.17
Otis College of Art and Design	3.26
San Francisco State University	3.31
California State University, Los Angeles (CSULA)	3.32
California State University, Northridge (CSUN)	3.37
Marist College	3.4
Louisiana State University	3.45
Washington State University	3.46
University of Rhode Island	3.56
University of the Incarnate Word	3.56
Oklahoma State University	3.59
Savannah College of Art & Design (SCAD)	3.6
University of Nebraska	3.6
Kent State University	3.61
Kansas State University	3.62
Oregon State University	3.62
Texas Tech University	3.63
University of Hawaii at Manoa	3.64
Syracuse University	3.67
California State University, Long Beach (CSULB)	3.68
Colorado State University, Ft. Collins	3.7
University of Cincinnati	3.7
University of North Carolina at Greensboro	3.7
Iowa State University	3.71
Dominican University	3.72
Virginia Commonwealth University	3.72
Michigan State University	3.74
Indiana University Bloomington	3.75
North Carolina State, Raleigh College of Design	3.81
Pratt Institute	3.82
University of Delaware	3.92
Virginia Polytechnic Institute and State University (Virginia Tech)	3.96
Auburn University	3.97
Washington University in St. Louis	4.21
Fashion Inst. of Tech (FIT)	N/A

School	Avg. GPA
Baylor University	N/A
California College of the Arts	N/A
Columbia College Chicago	N/A
Columbus College of Art & Design	N/A
Cornell University	N/A
Delaware State University	N/A
Drexel University	N/A
Fashion Institute of Design and Merchandising (FIDM)	N/A
Maryland Institute College of Art (MICA)	N/A
Moore College of Art & Design	N/A
Parsons - The New School	N/A
Rhode Island School of Design (RISD)	N/A
School of the Art Institute of Chicago (SAIC)	N/A
Stephens College	N/A
Thomas Jefferson University	N/A
University of Minnesota	N/A
University of North Texas	N/A
University of Texas, Austin	N/A
Massachusetts College of Art & Design (MassArt)	N/A 3.0 min. req.
Academy of Art University	N/A *Open admissions
Miami International University Art & Design	N/A *Open admissions

JOURNEY TO ART, DANCE, MUSIC, THEATRE, FILM, AND FASHION SERIES

JOURNEY TO
Fashion Design
COLLEGE ADMISSIONS & PROFILES

RACHEL A. WINSTON, PH.D.

JOURNEY TO
Fashion Merchandising
COLLEGE ADMISSIONS & PROFILES

RACHEL A. WINSTON, PH.D.

JOURNEY TO
Costume Design & Technical Theatre
COLLEGE ADMISSIONS & PROFILES

RACHEL A. WINSTON, PH.D.

JOURNEY TO
Theatre and the Dramatic Arts
COLLEGE ADMISSIONS & PROFILES

RACHEL A. WINSTON, PH.D.

JOURNEY TO
Musical
Theatre
COLLEGE ADMISSIONS & PROFILES

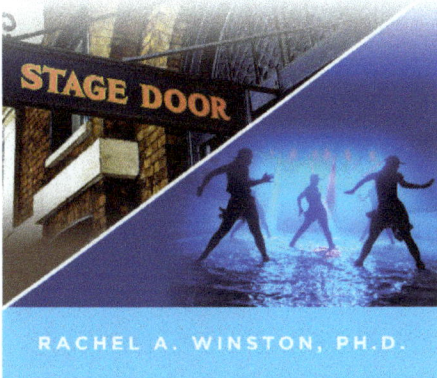

STAGE DOOR

RACHEL A. WINSTON, PH.D.

Live your dreams today remembering that discipline is the bridge between dreams and achievement!

"We believe in the American Dream that all people rich or poor can go as far in life as their talents and persistence will take them."
– Lizard Publishing Vision

At Lizard, we help you make your dreams come true.

CONTACT INFORMATION

Phone: 949-833-7706
E-mail: collegeguide@yahoo.com
Website: collegelizard.com and Lizard-publishing.com

COMPREHENSIVE HEALTH CARE SERIES

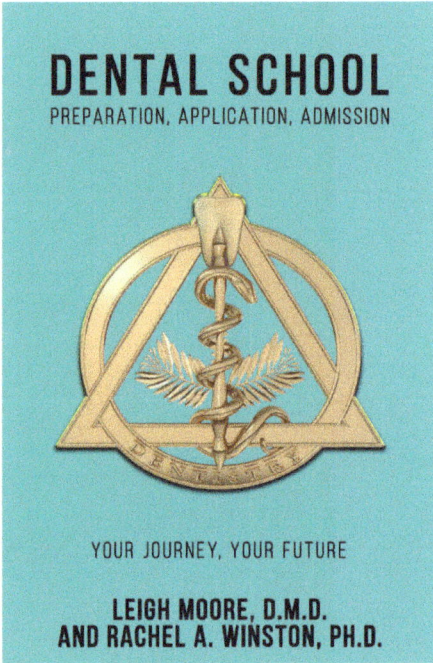

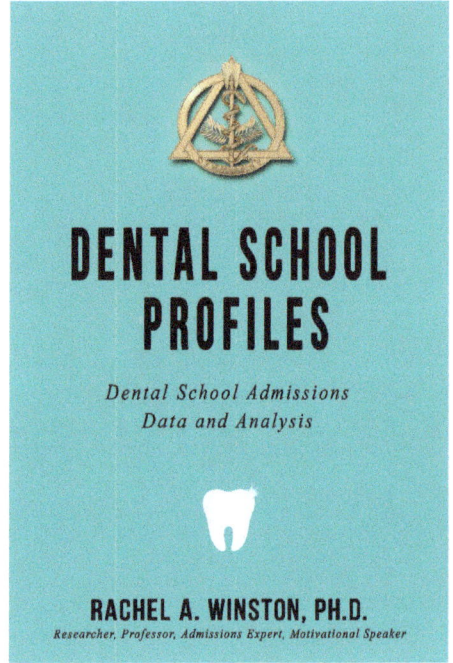

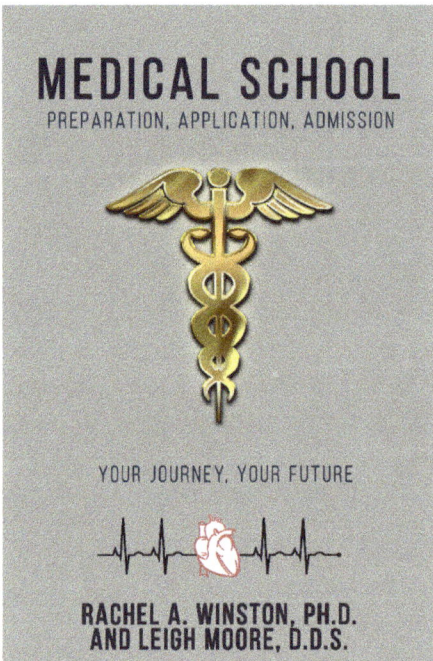

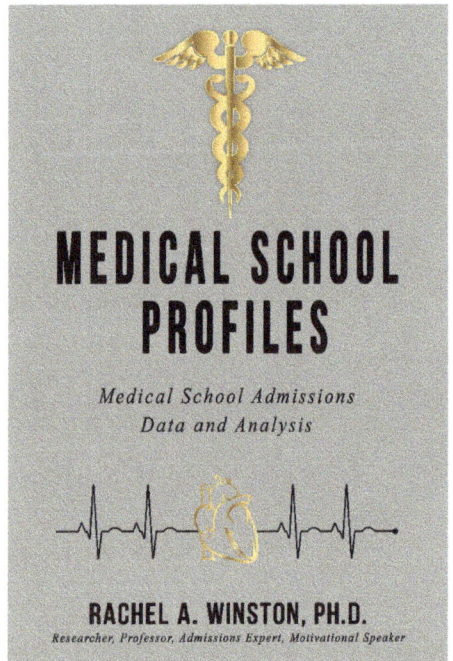

VET SCHOOL
PREPARATION, APPLICATION, ADMISSION

YOUR JOURNEY, YOUR FUTURE

RACHEL A. WINSTON, PH.D.
Researcher, Professor, Admissions Expert, Motivational Speaker

VET SCHOOL PROFILES

Veterinary Medical School Admissions Data and Analysis

RACHEL A. WINSTON, PH.D.
Researcher, Professor, Admissions Expert, Motivational Speaker

PHYSICIAN ASST. (PA) SCHOOL
PREPARATION, APPLICATION, ADMISSION

YOUR JOURNEY, YOUR FUTURE

RACHEL A. WINSTON, PH.D.
Researcher, Professor, Admissions Expert, Motivational Speaker

PHYSICIAN ASST. SCHOOL PROFILES

P.A. School Admissions Data and Analysis

RACHEL A. WINSTON, PH.D.
Researcher, Professor, Admissions Expert, Motivational Speaker

PHARM.D. SCHOOL
PREPARATION, APPLICATION, ADMISSION

YOUR JOURNEY, YOUR FUTURE

RACHEL A. WINSTON, PH.D.
Researcher, Professor, Admissions Expert, Motivational Speaker

PHARM.D. SCHOOL PROFILES

Pharmacy School Admissions Data and Analysis

RACHEL A. WINSTON, PH.D.
Researcher, Professor, Admissions Expert, Motivational Speaker

OSTEOPATHIC MEDICAL SCHOOL
PREPARATION, APPLICATION, ADMISSION

YOUR JOURNEY, YOUR FUTURE

RACHEL A. WINSTON, PH.D.
Researcher, Professor, Admissions Expert, Motivational Speaker

OSTEO SCHOOL PROFILES

Osteopathic Medical School Admissions Data and Analysis

RACHEL A. WINSTON, PH.D.
Researcher, Professor, Admissions Expert, Motivational Speaker

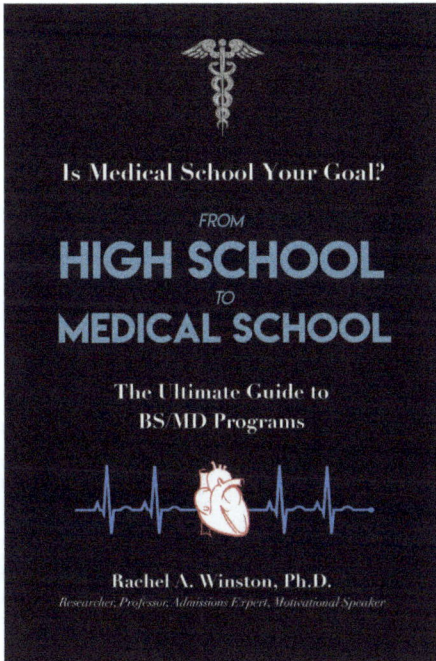

This comprehensive healthcare series is designed in full color to aid the growing number of applicants seeking clear, comprehensive materials. As a college admissions expert and former UCLA College Counseling Certificate Program faculty member, Dr. Winston is dedicated to helping students obtain the information they need.

FOR MORE INFORMATION

bsmdguide.com

medschoolexpert.com

Purchase books at Lizard-publishing.com

SERVICES OFFERED BY LIZARD EDUCATION:

- College Counseling
- Admissions News/Resources
- Essay Support and Editing
- Interview Preparation
- Road Trips to Visit Colleges
- Career Planning/Majors/Resumes
- BS/MD, BS/DO, BS/JD, BS/DDS
- Medical School
- Graduate School (Masters & Doctorate)
- Film Studio and Editing
- Portfolio Assistance/SlideRoom
- Athletics Recruiting/Highlight Films
- International Admissions/Visa/TOEFL
- Financial Aid and Scholarships
- UCs, Ivy Leagues, and Colleges Nationwide
- Book Publishing
- Engineering, Robotics, STEM
- Art Portfolios

Email: collegeguide@yahoo.com

Website: collegelizard.com

LIZARD

INDEX

Symbols

D

G

H

I

N

O

P

Q

R

T

U

V

W

X

Y

Z